Healthy Schools Healthy Lives

A Teacher's Guide to Tackling Childhood Obesity

Anita Loughrey

HOPSCOTCH

A division of MA Education Ltd

HOPSCOTCH

Published by
Hopscotch, a division of MA Education,
St Jude's Church, Dulwich Road,
London SE24 0PB
www.hopscotchbooks.com
020 7738 5454

© 2009 MA Education Ltd.

Written by Anita Loughrey
Book designed and illustrated by Emma Squire,
Fonthill Creative, 01722 717057

ISBN 978 1 90539 057 1

Foreward

At the start of 2008 in Healthy Weight, Healthy Lives: a Cross-Government Strategy for England (Department of Health/ Department for Children, Schools and Families 2008) the Prime Minister, Gordon Brown stated:

"Our ambition is to be the first major nation to reverse the rising tide of obesity and overweight in the population by ensuring that everyone is able to achieve and maintain a healthy weight. Our initial focus will be on children: by 2020, we aim to reduce the proportion of overweight and obese children to 2000 levels."

The concern in the media and simple observation of children and adults in shopping centres, schools and on the beach sustains this concern, yet the critical reader might query if obesity is really increasing and if it is a problem.

Up to date national statistics (NHS Information Centre 2006), using well accepted measurement criteria, indicate a third of children are overweight or obese. Children who are obese at 16 have a strong, but not inevitable risk of adult obesity (Viner and Cole 2006). Adult obesity is linked with disease such as certain cancers, diabetes and heart diseases which will put pressure on health services as well as challenge the people concerned. While difficulties in the future are of concern for the individual and the wider society, for the obese child the problems are of today. They may not be able to take part in activities with their peers, or at least not keep up with them and they are likely to be on the receiving end of teasing and bullying, which all impacts on their emotional well being at a time.

Childhood obesity is an issue that involves more than just the child. The government in Healthy Weight, Healthy Lives talked of developing policy areas that sought to promote children's health; to promote healthy food; to build physical activity into lives; to support health at work and to provide effective treatment and support when people become obese. Working within the ethos of such policy validates what many are doing and encourages others to go further. We need to be concerned with the environment in which children and young people live, the food that is advertised and made available to them and the physical activities with which they can be involved. Health workers are, and will be further, involved in the prevention of obesity, the identification of those becoming overweight and working with those who want to address their obesity. Promoting health (in its widest sense) of the whole school community involves considering the school food policy; the personal, social and health education programme as well as the facilities and opportunities for physical education and movement; all of which have the potential to make an impact on childhood obesity.

Education undertaken in an interactive manner, which is relevant to the child, family and those with whom they live is crucial. The government, through the Department of Health, took this up through Change4Life, a society-wide movement that aimed to prevent people from becoming overweight by encouraging them to eat better and move more (DH 2008).

Childhood Obesity promotes an educational approach and describes to those who work with children, whether they are teachers, health workers or from voluntary organisations, the current worrying situation. The text provides a variety of activities that will help children take an interest in, and responsibility for, their own nutrition and exercise. In doing this it provides vital material that will be useful in the wider strategy to address childhood obesity.

Val Thurtle
Programme Director Public Health Nursing (School Nursing and Health Visiting). University of Reading.

References

Department of Health/ Department for Children, Schools and Families (2008) Healthy Weight, Healthy Lives: a Cross-Government Strategy for England. London: HM Government

Department of Health (2008) Change4Life – Eat Well, Move More, Live Longer http://www.dh.gov.uk/en/News/Currentcampaigns/Change4Life/index.htm accessed 22.12.08

NHS Information Centre (2006) Health Survey for England 2005 Latest Trends. NHS Information Centre

Viner RM and Cole TJ (2006) Who changes body mass between adolescence and adulthood? Factors predicting change in BMI between 16 year and 30 years in the 1970 British Birth Cohort. International Journal of Obesity 30(9):1368-74.

With special thanks to Mary Stagg, Julie Conway, Sophia Ali and the staff of Spurcroft School, Thatcham.

Contents

The facts of childhood obesity

Obesity is a recognized disease. It has become a worldwide pandemic. The Government publication Healthy Weight, Healthy Lives: Guidance for Local Areas (March 2008) states that in the UK, "Almost two-thirds of adults and a third of children are overweight or obese."

The UK has the worst weight problem in Europe, with almost a quarter of adults classed as grossly overweight. Most worrying is the increase of obesity in children. Obesity rates have doubled among six-year-olds and trebled among 15-year-olds in the last ten years.

The World Health Organisation (WHO) calls obesity one of the greatest public health challenges of the 21st century on their website: www.euro.who.int/obesity.

By the International Obesity Taskforce's (IOTF) international standards nearly 22% of boys and 27.5% of girls aged 2-15 were found to be overweight in the UK. The IOTF analysis indicates a marked acceleration in the trend from the mid-1980s onwards.

The document Healthy Weight, Healthy Lives stresses that we will only succeed as a nation if the whole society plays a part. This is why child obesity has been included as a national priority within the NHS and why the Government launched a £75 million three-year marketing programme to promote healthy weight in the autumn of 2008. Schools have a big part to play in re-educating society.

It is important to highlight healthy eating and exercise in schools. By teaching the younger generation we will be helping to reduce the problem nationwide. It is easier to guide children toward good eating habits, sleeping and exercise routines when they are young. As they get older, they are strongly influenced by peer groups and advertising. This book aims to help schools, children and parents work together to improve overall health prospects and longevity of life.

Projects and initiatives

There are many projects and initiatives, which aim to promote healthy eating, exercise and emotional well-being. It is important primary schools are aware of these programmes.

"It is important to highlight healthy eating and exercise in schools. By teaching the younger generation we will be helping to reduce the problem nationwide."

National Healthy Schools Programme

A joint Department of Health (DH) and the Department for Children, Schools and Families (DCSF) initiative to combat the rise in obesity, is the National Healthy Schools Programme (NHSP). It aims to teach children the skills and knowledge to make informed health and life choices, so they are able to reach their full potential. This includes healthy eating and physical activity. The Government's target is for all schools to be participating in the NHSP by 2009 and aims for 75 percent of schools to have achieved National Healthy School Status.

In 2007, the Government agreed 198 national indicators to help local authorities prioritise their funding and set targets. Seven of these national indicators (NI) are directly linked to children and tackling obesity.

The National Child Measurement Programme

The National Child Measurement Programme (NCMP) was established in 2005 and is conducted by both the Department of Health (DH) and the Department for Children, Schools and Families (DCSF). Every year, as part of the NCMP, children in Reception and Year 6 are weighed and measured during the school year by the school nursing service and the results are made available to the children's parents.

The Tackling Obesities: Future Choices - Foresight Project maintains that giving the results to parents is a vital way of engaging both children and families about healthy lifestyles and weight issues. The figures have highlighted trends in growth patterns and obesity linked to particular areas and schools. This information is then used to inform local planning and the delivery of services for children.

Dcsf School Meal Standards

The Government has set down rules to maintain the standards of food being served within schools. The School Food Trust has launched a web-based tool that helps schools assess whether the food and drink provided at lunchtime and at other times of the school day meet these food-based standards. This is run in conjunction with the 'Million Meals' Campaign, which encourages the take-up of healthy school meals.

http://schoolfoodchecklist.schoolfoodtrust.org.uk/client/index.aspx

National Schools Fruit and Vegetable scheme

The School Fruit and Vegetable Scheme is part of the **5 A DAY** programme to increase fruit and vegetable consumption. Under the Scheme, all four to six year

National Indicator		Link to Tackling Obesity
N1 50	Emotional health of children	Overweight children are more likely to be bullied and suffer from low self-esteem. School-based interventions to reduce bullying are effective.
N1 52	Take up of school lunches	Encouraging more children to eat school dinners will ensure they get at least one healthy meal a day. This could improve nutritional intake and may reduce obesity.
N1 55	Obesity among primary school age children in Reception	Figures are being collated and analysed by the National Child Measurement Programme (NCMP)
N1 56	Obesity among primary school age children in Year 6	Figures are being collated and analysed by the National Child Measurement Programme (NCMP)
N1 57	Children and young people's participation in high quality PE and sport	Children should be doing at least 60 minutes of planned and incidental physical activity every day.
N1 69	Children who have experienced bullying	Schools can build good self-esteem through PSHE and Seal programmes
N1 198	Children travelling to school – mode of travel usually used	Schools can encourage pupils to walk and cycle to school to promote a healthier lifestyle.

old children in LEA maintained infant, primary and special schools will be entitled to a free piece of fruit or vegetable each school day.

This is the same scheme that was originally piloted and supported by lottery money in 2000. The Government took over the funding in March 2005 and expanded the scheme further. Now 99% of eligible schools have chosen to participate in the Scheme and nearly two million children receive a free piece of fruit or vegetable each school day.

The Mind, Exercise, Nutrition Do it (MEND) Programme

As a teacher, you will often be asked what is available for obese children and their parents outside of school. The MEND Programme is a fun, free after-school course which helps families to learn how to be fitter, healthier and happier. It was developed by experts in child health and supported by national lottery funding.

MEND Programmes are open to children aged 7 to 13 who are above their ideal weight. They must be accompanied by a parent or carer. There are currently MEND Programmes running in over 300 locations across the UK. More information is available at their website: www.mendprogramme.org

Change4Life initiative

This involves a series of adverts starting in January 2009 that promote healthy living. Firms including Cadbury, Unilever, Coca-Cola, Kellogg's, Kraft, Mars, Nestle and PepsiCo are all taking part alongside major supermarkets Asda, Tesco and The Co-operative Group. People will be able to call a dedicated helpline and speak to specially-trained advisors for advice on exercise, nutrition and support services. A website has also been set up to bring together more than 45,000 groups and projects aimed at promoting healthy living.

Anti-Bullying Week

This has been initiated by the Anti-Bullying Alliance, founded by NSPCC and National Children's Bureau (NCB), in 2002. The Alliance brings together over 50 organisations into one network with the aims of reducing bullying and ensuring teachers are equipped with the knowledge and skills to address bullying effectively. This includes a child being bullied over weight issues.

National School Meal Week

This is organised by the Food Standards Agency and provides a platform for school meals caterers to drive up school meal numbers as well as promote the importance of healthy eating to young children. By encouraging pupils to have a school dinner, we can ensure all children have at least one healthy meal a day.

National Lunchbox Week

Healthy eating starts at home with the family - according to the Schools Food Trust (SFT), less than 45% of primary and secondary school pupils eat school meals, resulting in more that half of all school children relying on lunchboxes and food from home. National Lunchbox Week (week commencing 1st September) has been set up by the snack manufacturer Sun Valley to support parents and offer advice and ideas to help them move away from fried and fatty snacks such as crisps and chocolate and find healthy and tasty alternatives.

Let's Get Cooking

Let's Get Cooking is a network of cookery clubs for young people and parents. The project received £20 million from the Big Lottery Fund. The money funds a potential 5,000 clubs, set up from Autumn 2007 and aims to ensure the next generation of children do not suffer from the same lack of cookery skills, which is currently contributing to the UK's emerging obesity crisis. www.letsgetcooking.org.uk

The Real Meals Cookbook

The Real Meals Cookbook is endorsed by top chef Phil Vickery and developed by the British Nutrition Foundation. It contains 32 classic recipes and sauces chosen by the public. The cookbook is available free to every Year 7 pupil in English secondary schools but can be purchased for £7.99 from teachernet online publications for schools. You can also download pdf's of some of the individual recipes. www.publications. teachernet.gov.uk

Wake and Shake Scheme

The Wake 'n' Shake programme is not mandatory but, has all ready proved itself to be a popular part of the school day in most primary schools. It encourages pupils to spring into action first thing each morning before lessons start for 5 – 10 minutes and again after lunch.

These Wake 'n' Shake sessions in the mornings and afternoons help to improve levels of concentration throughout the day.

The ten minute sessions are split into three sections and can be undertaken to music:

● Aerobics: The moves mainly use movement of the lower body to make the heart beat faster, warm up the body and prepare the children for the day ahead.

● Strength and mobilisation: This is aimed at strengthening the legs and increasing muscular endurance and interspersed with joint mobilisation exercises, encouraging flexibility and a full range of movement.

● Stretch and revitalise: The final section brings the heart rate back to normal, and stretches all the muscles that have been used to counter the effect of long periods of sitting down and hunching over desks, which can shorten the hamstring muscles and chest muscles.

Zonepark

Zonepark is led by the Lunchtime Staff who organise a range of sports for the children do throughout the week, such as netball, football, volleyball, rounders, skipping games, etc. This encourages the children to have an active lunchtime. This is also not a mandatory initiative but, contributes to tackling the obesity problem and meeting Government targets of 60 minutes of exercise a day, as specified in the New Performance Framework for Local Authority Partnerships: Single Set of National Indicators.

Huff and Puff

Everyone benefits from exercise. The Huff and Puff scheme encourages children to lead a healthier lifestyle by increasing activities on offer during break times. Children exchange a key ring that they have purchased at the office for play equipment. The money paid is used to purchase more equipment. The focus is on skills such as throwing, catching, hand/eye coordination, balance, cooperation, trust and team work. Lunchtime support staff and a selection of Year 6 children are trained to help ensure the scheme runs smoothly and the children become more active.

Determining obesity

Body Mass Index

The measurement used to determine whether a person's weight is within a healthy range is the Body Mass Index (BMI). Health workers use BMI because it compares weight against height. An adult is considered obese if they have a body mass index (BMI) of 30 kg/m2 or greater.

To work out a person's Body Mass Index:

Take their weight (kg) and divide it by the square of their height (m).
For example, if a person weighs 80kg and is 1.7m:
1. Multiply the height by itself 1.7x1.7=2.89
2. Divide the weight by this figure
3. 80 ÷ 2.89= 27.7kg/m2.
This gives a BMI of 27.7.

Once a child's BMI has been calculated, a chart is used to calculate whether they are overweight or obese. This chart takes into account the different growth rates between boys and girls as they get older.

Age (years)	OVERWEIGHT		OBESE	
	Boys	Girls	Boys	Girls
5	17.5	17.1	19.3	19.2
5.5	17.5	17.2	19.5	19.3
6	17.6	17.3	19.8	19.7
6.5	17.7	17.5	20.2	20.1
7	17.9	17.8	20.6	20.5
7.5	18.2	18.0	21.1	21.0
8	18.4	18.3	21.6	21.6
8.5	18.8	18.7	22.2	22.2
9	19.1	19.1	22.8	22.8
9.5	19.5	19.5	23.4	23.5
10	19.8	19.9	24.0	24.1
10.5	20.2	20.3	24.6	24.8
11	20.6	20.7	25.1	25.4
11.5	20.9	21.2	25.6	26.1
12	21.2	21.7	26.0	26.7

Adapted from: Cole et al, 2000. British Medical Journal

Using the national Body Mass Index percentiles approach (adopted by the Department of Health) 30.3 % of boys and 30.7% of girls were overweight. These Department of Health statistics are available to be seen and studied on the website: http://www.official-documents.co.uk/document/deps/doh/survey02/hcyp/tables/hcypt159.htm

Waist Circumference

BMI does not take into consideration the issue of fat distribution. People with more muscle than average, such as athletes, might be classified as overweight according to BMI, so the waist circumference measurement is also used to indicate whether or not they are at risk. The waist circumference measurement is taken at the mid-point between the lower rib and upper pelvis.

Research and statistics

The aim of this book is not to weigh you down with the research and figures. But, it is important to be aware of what is happening, as this information can be used to support your teaching.

UK Department of Health figures in the Government publication Healthy Weight, Healthy Lives show around one in three children between the ages of 2 and 15 are overweight. While in total more girls than boys are overweight, a greater number of boys are obese.

The International Obesity Taskforce research published in spring 2006, suggested that almost two million UK school children are overweight and 700,000 are obese. The study showed more than a quarter of girls and over a fifth of boys were identified as being obese, which means the number of obese children has tripled over twenty years.

Childhood obesity will have a knock on affect on a person's weight during adulthood. Government statistics show that children are more likely to have a weight problem if one parent is overweight, and the risk is increased if both parents are overweight or obese. In the UK 22% of men and 23% of women are obese.

The Department of Health predicts that if the current trend continues, by 2010 around 6.6 million men will be obese compared to 6 million women. Where there is obesity, there is a risk to health. Based on current trends, obesity will become the most common preventable cause of death.

The National Audit Office estimates that being obese can reduce lifespan by up to 9 years. In England alone, obesity is all ready responsible for about 9000 premature deaths per year.

This large rise in the amount of people being diagnosed as obese is a result of a mixture of genetic, behavioural and environmental factors.

"Childhood obesity will have a knock on effect on a person's weight during adulthood."

Genetic factors that can cause obesity

There are many genetic conditions that can cause obesity. As a teacher, it is important that you are aware if any child in your care suffers from any of these medical conditions. This is particularly important if you work within the special education schools.

Sensitivity to a child's feelings and personal situation should be adhered to. If a child has a medical problem that causes them to be overweight or obese, it is more than likely they would have been advised by their doctors and a dietician on how to manage their condition to help with the weight problem.

Medical reasons for obesity include:

Bardet Biedl Syndrome
This is a genetic disorder resulting in obesity that is usually limited to the trunk of the body. Many individuals are also shorter than average and suffer from severe retinal degeneration. There is no treatment available but, researchers have identified twelve genes linked to Bardet-Biedl syndrome, giving clear targets for treatment development.

Borjesson-Forssman-Lehmans Syndrome
Borjesson-Forssman-Lehmans Syndrome is a very rare condition where the baby is born obese and very floppy. During childhood they will experience problems with intelligence, epilepsy and facial disfigurement. Special education is required from an early age and adults require a variable degree of supervision. In some cases it can be treated with testosterone supplements.

Cohen Syndrome (Pepper Syndrome)
This is an inherited disorder that results in obesity. It is characterised by developmental delay, mental retardation, small head size (microcephaly), and weak muscle tone (hypotonia). Obesity often develops in late childhood or adolescence. When obesity is present, it typically develops around the torso, with the arms, hands, legs and feet remaining slender. There is no treatment.

Cushing's Syndrome
Cushing's syndrome is a hormonal disorder caused by prolonged exposure of the body's tissues to high levels of the hormone cortisol. This can be due to tumours in the pituitary gland or because they take glucocorticoid hormones such as prednisone for asthma, rheumatoid arthritis, lupus and other inflammatory diseases, or for

immunosuppression after transplantation. Symptoms vary, but most people have upper body obesity, rounded face, increased fat around the neck, and thinning arms and legs. Children tend to be obese with slowed growth rates. This condition is sometimes called 'hypercortisolism' and is relatively rare. Treatment depends on the specific reason for cortisol excess and may include surgery, radiation, chemotherapy or the use of cortisol-inhibiting medicine.

Froehlich Syndrome

Often referred to as Adiposogenital Dystrophy, this is a rare childhood metabolic disorder caused by tumours in the hypothalamus or pituitary gland, which increases appetite. It is characterised by the underdevelopment of the genitalia and is more commonly found in males. There has been some research into treatment using human chorionic gonadotropin, a glycoprotein hormone normally produced by a developing placenta.

Hypothyroidism (under-active thyroid)

This is where the thyroid gland, located in the neck, produces too little of the thyroid hormone, thyroxin, which regulates metabolism. Too little thyroxin slows the metabolism causing weight gain. This can be quite common in children. A blood test can be done to check hormone levels and the condition can be treated with tablets.

Insulinoma

An insulinoma is a tumour in the pancreas causing the production of excessive amounts of insulin, which in some cases may lead to obesity. Insulinoma are very rare in children, and if found it is more likely they have multiple areas of overactive insulin-secreting cells in the pancreas, rather than a single tumour. It is treated through surgery and medication.

Melanocortin 4 receptor Defect

This is a genetic disorder where a person is unable to store and use energy which results in becoming extremely obese. Mutations of the melanocortin-4 receptor (MC4R) gene are associated with up to 5.8% of monogenetic causes of obesity. There is no treatment but, education and maintaining a good diet can help prevent further medical complications.

Prader-Willi Syndrome

PWS is a complex genetic disorder present at birth, causing an insatiable appetite. Children with PWS require fewer calories than the typical child, which makes it harder to control their weight. The child may go to great lengths to get food, so parents and carers have to take strict measures to control food intake. As PWS is a genetic condition, it can not be cured, although, recent research has suggested treatment with growth hormone can help. It can be managed through good dietary control and educating the child.

Pseudohypoparathyroidism Type 1

This is an inherited disorder that causes many developmental problems, such as short stature and obesity. Some of these patients are not short during childhood, but due to a combination of factors, end up short as adults. Growth hormone deficiency has been identified as a contributing factor and research into whether growth hormone treatment can increase height (in children), reduce weight, and improve a variety of metabolic disturbances and overall health, is ongoing.

Syndrome X

Syndrome X is the name given to a set of symptoms which indicate that an individual may be suffering from what is called insulin resistance. This is a nutritional disease caused by not getting enough sleep, eating the wrong types of food and the body's inability to deal with the types of food eaten. Food high in glucose will trigger the pancreas to produce more insulin. Sleep deprivation prevents the replacement of essential hormones, which help regulate insulin levels. This can result in diabetes, hypertension and obesity. It occurs more often in young women.

> ## "Modern lifestyle often means we can end up eating too much and doing too little activity without even realising it."

The main treatment is to control sleep, diet and exercise. The mistake many people who are insulin resistant often make (and are encouraged to make) is to go on a strict calorie control diet with meal replacements in order to try to lose excess body fat. The problem with these sorts of diets is that they are unbalanced and often contain MORE sugar than the meals they replaced. Sufferers should consult a doctor and/or a dietician before making any dietary changes or starting an exercise program.

Behavioural and environmental factors that can cause obesity

Weight gain occurs when you eat more calories than you burn through physical activity. To lose weight a person needs to eat fewer calories, and burn more energy through physical activity. Modern lifestyle often means we can end up eating too much and doing too little activity without even realising it.

The IdeA and UKPHA health Significant Interest Event (SIG) held on 8th February 2008, identified we need to think about how we can change the urban environment to encourage physical activity. They state that, "New housing developments need to offer opportunities to bring together housing, schools, transport and work. This will help create environments that encourage active lifestyle. Moving people from public transport to walking and cycling is a key priority."

We need to increase everyday activity levels though the design of our villages, towns and cities, and to work out how to shift consumer purchasing patterns in favour of healthy options. They also highlighted that comprehensive licensing laws could help to tackle issues such as 'fast food' outlets near schools.

The government Foresight programme, established by David King, the chief scientific advisor and head of the Government Office for Science, did a two year study of obesity to improve our understanding of the causes of the world-wide epidemic. The study found in October 2007 the increasing prevalence of obesity is a consequence of modern life. They suggest that by 2050, in the UK about 60% of men, 50% of women and 25% of children will be obese. They project that the associated chronic health problems will cost society an additional £45.5 billion a year.

The Local Government Association (LGA) have been reported in the Daily Mail, Tuesday 7th October, 2008, to claim, "The epidemic could lead to a rise in council tax as public services – including transport and home care – are put under pressure. National Health Service figures revealed the cost of obesity to the NHS is set to soar by 50% to £6.3 billion in the next seven years."

Some of the behavioural and environmental factors that can lead to obesity include:

Caffeine
Caffeine is a stimulant and can disrupt sleep cycles, which disrupts hormone levels responsible for regulating body weight and metabolism. It can be found in many over the counter medicines, soft drinks and chocolate.

Comfort eating
It's easy to reach for a sugary pick-me-up when feeling stressed or upset whether you are an adult or a child. Chocolates and crisps can be replaced by healthy snacks such as, fruit and vegetables, and other low-calorie options such as plain popcorn, crackers and rice cakes. Children need to be educated to find ways to cope with stressful situations that don't involve food, such as exercising. It is a well known fact exercise helps promote mental well-being through the release of endorphins which can help make people less stressed and consequently less likely to want to comfort eat. This knowledge will help a child as they get older.

Electronic Devices - from computers, television to handheld game systems
More than ever, life for children seems to be spent sitting down. Spending a lot of time at a computer doing 'homework', playing computer games and watching television is contributing to an inactive lifestyle. Children should be encouraged to turn off their computer and get moving. In order to maintain a healthy weight, the New Performance Framework for Local Authority Partnerships: single set of National Indicators (2007) recommends 60 minutes of exercise a day.

Food labelled 'low-fat'
Low-fat foods contain high levels of sweeteners or sugar. High sugar foods will cause weight gain. It is important to read the labels and check the overall energy and calories. Although a food may have a reduced amount of fat, it may still have the same amount of calories.

Holidays
People not only tend to eat and drink more when they are on holiday but, they tend to eat out more. Portion sizes are often larger at restaurants or in takeaways. Children need guidance on the healthy options to pick in the buffet or restaurant. Small changes can be made such as asking for dressings in separate dishes so they can be added and incorporating activity into the holiday.

Lack of sleep
If a person does not get enough sleep their body will not produce enough of the necessary hormones required to regulate their metabolism. This can stimulate hunger and reduce energy levels, which will cause people to put on weight.

In these modern times, we regard sleep as a waste of time. But sleep is essential for good physical and mental health. You feel wonderful when you wake up from a good night's sleep. A child should have between ten and fourteen hours sleep, depending on their age.

Portion sizes
The size of portions served in restaurants and in supermarket packages has increased. A study by the World Cancer Research Fund (WCRF) found that burgers, for example, have doubled in size since 1980. If we are given a larger portion, we will automatically eat more.

Coping with larger portion sizes is a matter of simply stopping when we feel full. It takes up to 20 minutes for the body to let the brain know a person has eaten enough. If we eat slowly we have a better chance of avoiding that over-stuffed feeling. By cooking fresh, healthy meals at home, instead of eating out or buying supermarket ready meals, it is possible to save money whilst controlling portion sizes. It is important to re-educate people that it is acceptable to leave food on the plate if they are full.

Pause for thought

Parents can be very sensitive to their child being weighed. If you have overweight or obese children in your class you need to be extra careful and sensitive to their feelings. It is not advisable to weigh children or calculate BMI within the classroom environment, as some parents may complain.

At the Primary School level it is not really the child's fault if they are overweight or obese. Children need to be educated on healthy diet and healthy exercise routines but, ultimately parents and carers play a large contributing factor. Education is the first step to positively changing British attitudes to exercise and nutrition and creating a healthier society.

If a parent approaches you about their child being overweight or obese, there are ways you can help them tackle their child's weight problem. You can suggest they get advice and help from their family doctor, or the school nurse. A doctor may refer the family to a dietician who can help the parent's devise a healthy eating plan. The doctor might also recommend an exercise plan and the safest way to start out according to their child's individual needs. You could also draw their attention to the MEND Programme, which was outlined earlier in this chapter. This is a free initiative and runs after school hours.

It is important for teachers to emphasise that dieting by restricting calories is inappropriate, as children are still growing physically and mentally and will need adequate nutrition. For a healthy weight to be achieved and maintained the parents and child must understand the need for dietary changes and be informed and involved. Effective weight control programs should focus on eating healthy foods, increasing physical activity and getting sufficient sleep, not counting calories.

Point out it is easier to gain weight than to lose weight. Everyone involved should be aware that children learn by example, at home and at school. Teachers, parents and carers should set good examples in their own food choices and lifestyle. Consistent and regular support for the child and their family is needed for improvement to occur. Everyone's cooperation is vital to success.

The role of the school in obesity prevention

Obesity is the most common health problem facing children today and schools can be intrinsic in educating children and their parents on the importance of healthy eating and adequate exercise.

The role of the school is to teach good eating and exercise habits and to encourage both the children and their parents to adopt these ideas as part of their daily routines and lifestyles. Health Education starts from the moment a child enters school. The Foresight programme advocated in October 2007 that, we need policies aimed at different life stages, in particular early on to establish appropriate child growth, healthy eating and activity habits.

The statutory Framework for the Early Years Foundation Stage (EYFS) provide clear guidance to ensure teaching staff promote the good health of children and encourage positive attitude towards making healthy choices and engaging in physical activity.

The EYFS states that:
- Meals snacks and drinks provided for children must be healthy, balanced and nutritious

- Fresh drinking water must be available at all times.

- The physical development area of learning and development (one of six areas in the EYFS) states that children 'must be supported in developing and understanding of the importance of physical activity and making healthy choices in relation to food.'

These guidelines continue throughout a child's primary education and into secondary education.

Each school should identify a named member of staff who is responsible for ensuring health education is taught and that the relevant policies are put in place throughout the school. This person should preferably be from the senior management team with the authority to be able to deal with any issues of being obese or overweight arising from parents and specific children. He/she will require a job description.

A job description is not a definitive version of a particular post within the school but is rather an attempt to indicate an agreed responsibility. Each teacher is expected to take responsibility for at least one aspect of the school curriculum.

As a subject co-ordinator you would be expected to:

Have subject expertise:
- Have a wide knowledge of the specified subject area and current developments.

- Show enthusiasm for the subject .

- Find opportunities to promote the subject within the school.

- Develop and review policies.

Be responsible for resources:
- Manage and organise resources.

- Order resources as appropriate and check deliveries.

- Monitor the allocated budget.

Initiate staff training:
- Help other staff to develop the relevant subject knowledge.

- Lead inset/discussions at staff meetings.

- Recommend inset opportunities for staff.

Contribute to whole-school planning and record keeping:
- To advise on planning and record keeping .

- Maintain a yearly action plan.

Monitor:
- Monitor the subject throughout the school as appropriate.

- Report to governors as requested.

Maintain record keeping:
- Develop school portfolio as appropriate.

Taking this into consideration the specific key tasks for the school's Health Education Coordinator would include:
- Development of the health education curriculum from F1 to Y6.

- Serve as a liaison with the community health agencies to provide services within the school.

- Write policies relating to health issues and concerns for both employees and pupils.

- Ensure adequate Health Education resources are available for all teachers from F1 to Y6.

- Serve on committees and represent the school at meeting where health education is a topic of concern.

- Identify school training needs and provide school-based training as required.

- Have knowledge of the latest trends, research and concerns in the area of health education.

- Have knowledge of the organisation and procedures of the social welfare agencies.

- Apply principles of conflict resolution to resolve interpersonal problems that may arise.

- Work effectively with the SMT, teachers and other members of staff to improve the health education curriculum.

Staff as role models

It is inevitable that many members of staff will also have weight issues. They may be overweight, obese or underweight. Staff awareness of weight issues is ultimately important. It is unreasonable to expect children to look at and possibly change their behaviour if the teacher is unwilling to examine and change their own behaviour.

We should all:

1. Walk the walk and talk the talk by eating healthfully and seeking to enjoy eating that way, as well as getting sufficient exercise.

2. Promote healthy school breakfasts and lunches, school snacks, and school party foods.

3. Teach or facilitate others to teach about nutrition in a meaningful way, both formally and informally.

4. Support the physical education curriculum and promote active lunchtime recess and active play after school.

5. Counsel and / or refer overweight children, which will include involving families.

(*Annette Lavalle, RN, MPS, US school nurse and pioneer in obesity treatment and prevention.*)

This is excellent advice and should be adhered to throughout all UK schools. Adults (teachers, parents, school nurses) must act as role models. This is critical to success of any weight management program. The NHS Department of Health research indicates that it's not what adults say that makes a difference, it's what they do; if we want our children to eat more vegetables then we need to eat more vegetables. If we want them to exercise, we need to exercise.

The issue of weight should be addressed as a whole school and provisions should be made for staff to raise the issue of obesity that takes account of their own weight status. This should include the staff sitting

and eating with the children to model healthy food choices and good manners, as well as being physically involved in the school's Wake and Shake sessions and PE lessons, by warming up with the children and demonstrating good technique.

Adopting a whole school approach

In order for the whole school to be working together toward the same goals to combat childhood obesity there must be certain policies in place that the whole school adhere to.

These policies are:
- The School Food Policy

- PE curriculum / policy

- Food technology policy

- Science policy

- (PSHE and Citizenship) Emotional health and wellbeing policy

The policies need to:
- Support whole school improvement

- Have clear aims and objectives

- Support the teaching learning and practice of healthy eating and drinking by outlining the resources available

- Ensure pupil safety

- Include pupils in the decision making process both individually and through school council

- Support continual staff development

- Encourage school home-links which are essential for long-term success

- Outline opportunities for pupils' achievements to be celebrated

Example of a Whole School Food Policy Aim

To ensure all aspects of food and drink are promoted and taught throughout the whole school

Objectives
- To provide the necessary information for pupils to make healthy choices about food and drink

- To ensure consistent messages are given about healthy eating and drinking

- To promote health awareness

- To establish good eating and drinking habits for life

- To support good practice by ensuring clear links between the curriculum and the provision of food in school

Drinks

The school endeavours to ensure clean drinking water is available for pupils and staff throughout the school day. Providing drinking water in school helps pupils and teachers concentrate.

Children are also encouraged to bring in a bottle of plain water from home, which is stored in a designated place within the classroom for easy access when they require a drink. Children are regularly reminded to drink water after break and more frequently during hot weather to establish good practice for future drinking habits.

Bottles should be taken home at the end of the school day to be washed and bought back with clean, fresh water the following day. If children are unable to bring a water bottle, water is available from the school water fountains.

The school actively discourages the consumption of sugary and fizzy drinks on the school premises or on school trips. Research has shown that drinking plain water promotes concentration, increases attainment and helps prevent tooth decay.

Lunch

The school is committed to providing a welcoming eating environment that encourages positive social interaction and healthy eating. School meals are provided by contracted school caterers, who follow the Dcsf School Meal standards. A menu of food choices is provided and includes a vegetarian option each day. The caterers also provide regular theme days.

The school provides information and advice for parents and carers on what to include as part of a packed lunch. It is requested they do not include sweets and fizzy drinks. Rewards will be given to pupils for good meal time etiquette and behaviour and for making healthy food choices.

Snacks

Only fruit and vegetables will be consumed during break times as snacks. KS1 are entitled to a free piece of fruit or vegetable each day as part of the 5 a day National School Fruit and Vegetable Scheme, as outlined in Chapter One.

Food across the curriculum

As part of our goal towards teaching our pupils good habits to maintain a healthy lifestyle we have ensured that issues on maintaining a healthy diet is taught through a wide range of cross-curricular links, to provide a consistent message across the whole of the curriculum.

- **Literacy** provides children with the opportunity to explore poetry, persuasion, argument and narrative work using food and food-related issues as a stimulus.

- **Maths** can offer the possibility of understanding nutrition labelling, calculating quantities for recipes, weighing and measuring ingredients.

- **Science** provides an opportunity to learn about the types of food available, their nutritional composition, digestion and the function of different nutrients in contributing to health, and how the body responds to exercise.

- **RE** provides the opportunity to discuss the role of particular foods in the major religions of the world. Children experience different foods associated with religious festivals.

- **ICT** enables pupils to research food issues using the internet and other electronic resources.

- **Food Technology** as part of the D+T curriculum provides the opportunity to learn about healthy eating through practical work with food, including preparation and cooking to promote good practice that will benefit the children for life. Pupils' safety when undertaking practical work with food is carefully monitored and a member of staff has attained a certificate in Food Hygiene.

- **PSHCE** encourages young people to take responsibility for their own health and well-being, teaches them how to develop a healthy lifestyle and addresses issues such as body image. PSHCE is taught throughout the curriculum and through circle-time and assemblies.

- **Geography** provides an opportunity to learn where food comes from and to focus on the natural world and changing environment, offering the chance to consider the impact our consumer choices have on people across the world that rely on growing food as their source of income.

- **History** provides insight into changes in diet and food over time.

- **Physical Education** provides pupils with the opportunity to develop physically and to understand the practical impact of sport, exercise and other physical activity such as dance and walking and how both healthy eating and regular exercise is important to maintain a good body weight.

- **RE** includes discussions on the role of food in religion and religious festivals.

- **Extra-curricular activities** such as cookery and gardening clubs will promote good hygiene and healthy eating. All out-of-school events will take into consideration the Whole School Food Policy in the range of refreshments on sale to the children.

SEN

Information and photographs of children with allergies are kept in the school office and staff room. The Special Needs Register maintains a record of pupils with allergies and special dietary needs, including pupils who have been diagnosed as overweight or obese.

Partnership with parents and carers

A good partnership between home and school is essential to ensure the success of the Whole School Food Policy. Parents and carers are kept informed and regularly advised about healthy eating through leaflets and the school newsletter.

Role of the Governors

The governors monitor and check that the school policy is upheld and offer guidance to parents if necessary.

Monitoring and review

The Headteacher and Health Education Coordinator will monitor and review the Whole School Food Policy annually to take account of new developments.

Class activities

There are three key components of obesity prevention. These are diet, physical activity and getting enough sleep. Weight cannot be lost and maintained without attention to all three of these areas.

Included in the next two sections are a variety of classroom activities with photocopiable worksheets. It is not intended that you use them all as some will cover the same concepts from a different angle but, they could be used throughout the whole school from Key Stage One to Key Stage Two or for differentiation within the classroom. All the activities can be built upon and adapted for your own purposes.

Effects of obesity to motivation and self-esteem

Obesity can have a detrimental effect on emotional well-being. There are links between obesity, low self-esteem and underachievement in school. Many emotional problems occur from feelings of inferiority and bullying from classmates. Overweight children who have the lowest self-esteem were found to have parents who teased them about their weight problems.

Being bullied about weight can be a vicious circle, as it often leads to comfort eating. However, telling someone they should consider the long term effects and food is not going to make them feel better in the long run does not help. A child needs to understand why the food is not going to make them ultimately happy and have something to replace the need for immediate comfort.

How much being overweight affects a child is dependent on perceptions, and on the culture in which they grow up. Some parents and cultures are more accepting of a wider range of weights than others. But parents should be made aware that obesity is detrimental to health.

Perceived amount of overweight is actually a better predictor of self-esteem than actual body weight. Research has shown children tend to become conscious of their weight from around the age of eight onwards. It is rare for very young children to be overly conscious about their weight.

Children who view themselves as overweight are more likely to be unhappy about their weight condition. Some of those children may be obese and others may be just a few pounds overweight, but consider themselves to have a serious problem. Girls are more dramatically affected by weight and perceived weight problems than boys.

Moderate exercise has been proved to reduce depression and increase levels of self-esteem. Opportunities to discuss their feelings also help counteract low self-esteem. This is why it is important for an obese child to have the opportunity to speak to someone about how they feel.

Someone who feels good about themselves tends to be socially more skilful and more accepted by others.

Ideas for promoting self-esteem

Circle time activities are an excellent way to discuss issues as a whole class and help to improve self-esteem if carried out regularly and with empathy. They can be used with children of any age but the activity should be geared at the correct level for the class. They are not as successful as a one-off activity.

Children should sit in a circle without tables and desks to act as a barrier. The teacher should also take the opportunity to get involved and take a turn in the activity. It is important to discuss and agree the rules before you start. Rules should include respecting each other and that only one person should speak at a time, which can be facilitated with a 'talking object' to pass around the circle if desired. The teacher should set the tone by taking every opportunity to make positive comments. The aim is to emphasise positive qualities about everyone.

The activities below are not specifically related to being overweight or obese but, help create a strong bonded class that will be more receptive to dealing with bigger issues. The activities should be ongoing and only need last a couple of minutes.

Discussion Time

Non-controversial topics can encourage participation and create a positive ethos within the classroom and ultimately the whole school. Some ideas for discussion around the circle are:

● My favourite activity is…

- Being a friend means…

- The best day of my life was…

- The worst day of my life was…

- The best thing about the school is…

- The worst thing about school is…

Helping Hands

In the circle, discuss how they can help each other during the school day both in the classroom and the playground, at lunch and in assembly, etc. If everyone is in agreement with an idea presented to the circle, ask a child to write it down on a cut-out of a hand. Try to include helping people when they are sad, or hurt.

Put all the helping hands on a display board and when somebody in the class helps in one of the ways they can add their name to the hand. Ask if anyone wants to put up someone's name, at the end of the session. Clap or cheer for the children who succeed in getting their name written up.

Remind children about the helping hand board regularly and about helping each other. Congratulate the children when they get their name put on the board.

The Affirmation Game

To begin, hand out pieces of paper and ask the children to write their name on it. Collect all the names in, fold them up and place them in a tin (or other container) and mix them up.

Pick two names at random from the tin. The couple picked from the tin should then say something nice about each other. Explain not to simply say something about their clothes, especially if they are wearing school uniform but, to mention what they are like as a person. For example, I like X because he is kind, I think Y is a good person because she helps me with my maths, or is a good swimmer.

Aim to pick two or three pairs of names from the tin each time.

The Friendship Chain

To begin, hand out pieces of paper and ask the children to write their name on it, as for the affirmation game. You can use the same names as written previously if you've kept them.

Pick one name from the tin. Ask the child picked out of the tin to stand in the middle of the circle and to choose two people from the class. You could specify one male and one female person should be chosen if you wish. Ask these two children to stand up and say 'X is a good friend because…'. Each time check with the first child to see if they are happy with the statement they have heard.

These two children remain in the circle and hold hands, either side of the first child. They then get to pick one person each who will come into the circle and join the chain. They need to say, 'Y or Z (being the person who chose them) is a good friend because…'. Again, the child who picked them should be happy with the statement they have heard.

Aim to repeat this process about four or five times at most, else the chain gets too long.

What is Bullying?

Ask the children to suggest things they think are bullying such as, name calling, hitting, taking friends away. List their ideas. Then ask them to suggest words which describe how this behaviour would make someone being bullied feel and make a separate list. Finally, ask them how they think bullying should be dealt with, such as a telling-off, missing break times, etc.

Use this method to reinforce school rules and explain that telling a teacher or other member of staff is not telling tales but will ultimately make the school a safer place. Stories about bullying can be used to stimulate discussion.

Dealing with bullying

Bullying can be defined as deliberate, hurtful behaviour, repeated over a period of time. Obese children can often be victims of bullying and if it occurs at your school the issue must be addressed.

The three main types of bullying are:

- Physical (hitting, kicking, spitting, damage to property, theft).

- Verbal (name calling).

- Indirect (exclusion, spreading rumours).

Prejudice towards obesity is one of the main reasons for bullying within schools. Overweight children are often viewed as less valued and inferior to others in educational and social terms. This opinion is unfortunately reinforced by the media.

Research reveals boys and girls bully in different ways. Girls are more likely to use exclusion from friendships, rumour spreading, gossip and name calling, whilst boys are more likely to use physical force to intimidate their victims. Research has shown obese children are often likely to be the perpetrators of bullying, in order to divert attention away from being bullied themselves and regain a feeling of control. It is a well known fact that people who are bullied will begin to exhibit bullying behaviour themselves.

Studies prove that school-based interventions to reduce bullying are effective. Circle time activities are a good way to discuss the effects of bullying and what bullying is but, they are not an appropriate forum to deal with specific issues of bullying.

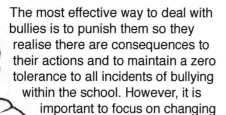

The most effective way to deal with bullies is to punish them so they realise there are consequences to their actions and to maintain a zero tolerance to all incidents of bullying within the school. However, it is important to focus on changing the bully's behaviour and avoid negative labelling.

The child's parents or carers need to be involved to help change the attitude of the child. Time should be spent talking to the child who has bullied to explain why their actions were inappropriate and they should be encouraged to change their behaviour in future.

In extreme cases, where these initial discussions have proven ineffective, the Headteacher should inform the Governors of the school, and may consider contacting external support agencies, such as social services. Intimidation, harassment and assault are offences, whatever the age of the perpetrator, or the victim.

Every incident of bullying is unique and will need to be investigated. Bystanders' testimonies are vital to determining what occurred. Again the teacher needs to reinforce that telling someone what has happened is not telling tales but will ultimately make the school a safer place.

A child who has been the victim of bullying should be offered an immediate opportunity to discuss the experience with a member of staff of their choice. They should be reassured that the school is going to do everything in its power to ensure it will never happen again and the child should be offered continuous support to restore their self-esteem and confidence.

Awareness of the nature of bullying and the school's no tolerance policy can be raised through drama, assemblies and PSHE lessons.

Buddy system

The 'buddy system' is where a child is selected to befriend a pupil who is new to the school, or having difficulties. This can be done within the classroom, or often older children in the school are appointed to help younger children with problems during break times. The system works well if the selection process is carefully thought out and the 'buddy' is given some specific rules to follow. The teacher needs to check its effectiveness regularly and deal with concerns promptly.

Studies have shown the buddy system is a positive way to prevent incidents of bullying before they

escalate. The buddy can raise awareness of bullying as it occurs, deter bullies from picking on another child as someone else is present and it also promotes positive friendships.

School's anti-bullying policy

It is a Government requirement for all schools to have an anti-bullying policy. The aim of the policy should be to ensure every child can learn in a secure and caring environment where bullying is regarded as unacceptable. The policy should show the school is able to recognise signs of bullying and will act promptly and firmly against all forms of bullying.

> ### "A child who has been the victim of bullying should be offered an immediate opportunity to discuss the experience with a member of staff of their choice."

The policy should outline the school's procedure for dealing with bullying. If bullying is suspected or reported, the incident should be dealt with immediately by the member of staff who has been approached. If a parent has approached the teacher, they should be reassured the matter will be dealt with very seriously. An appointment should be made for the parent to discuss the matter further once the teacher has been able to investigate. It is important to interview the victim, the bully and anybody else who may have seen the incident.

A clear account of the incident should be recorded and given to the Headteacher, who should be kept informed at all stages. If the matter can not be resolved by the class teacher it may need to be referred to the Headteacher, Deputy or a designated member of the Senior Management Team. Class teachers and parents should be kept informed. Sanctions should be used as appropriate and in consultation with all parties.

The policy should be reviewed annually to assess its implementation and effectiveness. It is important that the anti-bullying policy is continually evaluated and monitored to ensure it is achieving its aims.

Anti-bullying Audit Tool

It is possible to build a picture of the nature and extent of bullying within the school by carrying out a bullying questionnaire. This will help check whether the school's policies and procedures are working. There is an excellent survey available at: *http://www. anti-bullyingalliance.org.uk/Page.asp?originx_4237co_ 4721421398769u17h_2007627412x*

Pause for thought

Teachers will notice that parents who have overweight children are more concerned about them being bullied than the fact their child is obese. The parents have a greater concern about the bullying factor rather than the overall health of their child because they are looking at the short-term consequences rather than the long-term effects.

The obese child needs to break the cycle of comfort eating when they are upset, angry and distressed, which may be accentuated by being bullied. More care will be needed when offering the chid support. It may be necessary to point out to parents the effects to the child's physical health and that there is a need for a healthy diet and increased physical activity.

Explain if sweets and fatty foods are not available, then the issue of denying them will not occur. If the choice of things to eat only includes healthy foods, then the child will eat the healthy things on offer.

Suggest parents try after-school clubs like gymnastics or ballet, or go swimming together to help raise self-esteem and make the child more active. Explain how walking to school together, rather than driving, will provide a very good opportunity for parent and child to chat. Emphasise that their children should go to bed at a reasonable time and get between ten and fourteen hours sleep a night (depending on their age) to raise energy levels and help replenish the necessary hormones to burn off excess fat. If they establish good food, exercise and sleep habits now they will last into adulthood.

Partnership with parents in preventing obesity

Schools need to encourage a whole family approach to eating well and being active because parental support is paramount to tackling childhood obesity. Any interventions aimed at preventing childhood obesity must involve the parents. The parents are an essential factor for change, not only in their children's behaviour but also in their attitude.

Research and statistics

The Government publication, Healthy weight, healthy lives: guidance for local areas (March 2008) states:

"Given the important influence parents have over their children's behaviour, any interventions aimed at children will have to adopt a family-centred approach to changing behaviour. Research shows that parents are extremely sensitive to their children being labelled as obese or overweight and so being stigmatised or bullied, which could result in poor self-esteem. Teachers need to be aware of these issues and know how to work with overweight and obese children and their families. This includes being able to identify them, raising the issue of weight and providing information and advice, as well as signposting and referring on to services as appropriate while avoiding stigmatising the child."

It is estimated that one in 5 children aged between two-years and fifteen-years-old in England will be obese by 2010. The Department of Health warn that many parents still do not understand the dangers associated with being obese and the threats it has on a person's health. A survey commissioned by the department revealed just 12% of parents with overweight children knew their child was fatter than they should be. Only 38% were aware that obesity could lead to heart disease, while 6% knew of a link between being overweight and cancer.

Parents need advice on what they should be feeding their children due to mixed messages from the media and a limited understanding of correct food nutrition. For this reason, the Department of Health have produced three leaflets entitled, Why Weight Matters, Your Weight, Your Health and Why Your Child's Weight Matters. These are available free the DH Publications Orderline: www.dh.gov.uk/publications.

Parents need to reconsider what they cook, what they buy, what they give as snacks and how they keep their children occupied. It is a lifestyle change.

Advice for parents

If asked by parents how they can help their child to lose weight it is wise to emphasise the child should be involved at each step of the discussion. Parents of obese children should allow them to guide their own treatment.

There are five important issues teachers can discuss with parents:

- **WHY?** Why does the child want to lose weight? Is it a problem they have identified, or has a teacher, doctor or health worker bought it to the parent's attention, or has the parent recognised there is a problem? The reason behind the child wanting to lose weight is the driving force behind their potential success so it is important for parents to discuss this with the child. Any discussion about the need to lose weight should be approached in a sensitive, caring way. A weight loss programme will only be effective for life if the child is motivated to lose weight. They have to want it themselves, not because they are told this is what they are going to do but because they understand the long-term benefits of losing weight.

- **WHEN?** If the child has been diagnosed as obese parents should ensure their child starts a weight loss programme straight away – not tomorrow, or next week, or after Christmas. Parents can help their child identify any potential barriers they might face in making a commitment to lose weight by encouraging them to make a list of the things that might stop them achieving their goals and discuss ways with them that they can overcome these problems. It is good to acknowledge past attempts at trying to lose weight but, it is not good to dwell on them. If a person expects to fail they will. Learn from the experiences and move on. Don't make excuses except it as a failure and resolve to change the reaction to a similar situation. It is impossible to move forward if the child is stuck in the past.

- **WHAT?** What are the methods for successful weight loss? A sensible and sustainable eating plan, a regular bedtime routine and an increase in activity will lead to weight loss, but the child should be in control of these methods and the changes they make for success to be achieved. Ask the child to set their own target weight and guide them to make their own decisions about how they will achieve this. Parents can help think of activities their child enjoys to keep them motivated but they should be meaningful to the child. What motivates the parent may not have the same impact for the child. It is important for parents to remember that the child is in charge of the changes they make. But, with regular review and support, attainable targets, rewards, empathy, understanding and empowerment, children will be encouraged to continue and succeed in the long term, by knowing they're on the right track.

- **HOW?** It helps to record the child's target weight and interim targets, giving them a goal to aim for and commit to. Imagining the results of succeeding is a good motivator and helps to overcome any potential barriers. The child needs to set their own attainable goal. They need to understand it will be easier to aim for a little at a time. One pound every fortnight amounts to twenty pounds in a year. Parents need to ensure the child has targets that are realistic and achievable. Food should not be used as a reward and rewards should not be withheld as a punishment. Small frequent rewards work better than larger ones. It is also a good idea to make treats an activity based item, such as swimming, cycling or dancing. It is important to stick to the rules and ensure the reward matches the achievement made.

  Teachers can point parents in the direction of the NHS website Change 4 life www.nhs.uk/change4life, which contains useful information and ideas for parents to adopt a healthier lifestyle.

- **WHOM?** Involving at least one parent in a weight-loss process improves overall short- and long-term weight loss, as does overall support from family and friends. All family members must co-operate in order for children to succeed. Parents may be able to get advice from their doctor, health visitor or the school nurse. There are also free after school support groups like the MEND Programme which have trained staff who are able to support the obese child and their family. Working with other children who are experiencing similar hurdles to weight loss can be supportive and help a child to reach their goals.

Adopting a whole family approach

In order for an overweight or obese child to lose weight and stick to a healthy lifestyle, the whole family need to be working together toward the same goals. There must be certain agreements in place that the whole family adhere to. These may be difficult for everyone but to make progress an obese child needs to have the support and understanding of the rest of the family and everything suggested in this book will help everyone in the family become healthier and ultimately live longer lives.

Parents as role models

Obesity often runs in families, with one or both parents also being overweight or obese. This may be due to genetic factors but, is also because families tend to share eating, sleeping and physical activity habits. It is unrealistic to try to change one member of the family's behaviour whilst the other members are continuing to model bad habits that counteract the final goal of losing weight. Parents are role models and need to reinforce and support good eating, sleeping and exercise habits if progress is going to be made. Parents can

encourage their child by showing how enthusiastic they are about trying new foods, or to going for a walk or a swim.

During infancy parents establish the foundation for their child's food habits through exposure and repeated experience. The way parents feed their children contributes to individual differences in how well children can regulate their food intake and will influence how much energy their child has. Children should be given opportunities to taste a variety of healthy, nutritious foods from an early age. Parents should be willing to prepare fresh food and move away from processed pre-packaged meals.

At an early age, children will eat what their parents eat. If a parent turns their nose up at something the child will too. In this way, a parent's unhealthy eating behaviour will influence the development of being overweight in their children.

> **"Parents are role models and need to reinforce and support good eating, sleeping and exercise habits if progress is going to be made."**

Food can be an addiction and it is up to the whole family to break the habit. The whole family need to be motivated. Everyone needs to work together toward the same goal. This can be achieved by having a suitable reward when the goal is reached. The reward has to be something that is of interest to everyone in the family, such as a day trip or a holiday.

It is important to stress that in the same way teachers are role models at school, parents must act as role models at home. This is critical to success of any child weight management program.

Comfort eating

Parents have the biggest influence on their children's development of food-related behaviours, such as the desire for comfort eating. This is a bad habit formed from birth and begins with feeding on demand. Comfort eating is harder to modify in adults and so best tackled during childhood.

If parents ask for advice about ways to stop their child from comfort eating, you could suggest:
- Avoid using food as a reward as this can reinforce the idea of food as a source of comfort.

- Instead of having a fast-food meal to celebrate a good school report, for example, buy a gift, go to the cinema, or have a friend to stay overnight.

- Instead of giving food to comfort a child when they are upset parents could give attention, hugs and listen.

The child should be persuaded to consider the long-term effects of eating comfort food. They need to realise eating is not going to make them feel better in the long run. The food is not making them ultimately happy. As a family it is important to discuss why they are treating themselves with food. Are they hungry? Does it make them feel better?

Snacking

Children can not be expected to know what foods are good for them unless they have been taught. The child is not the person with the buying power. The parents have to be the ones strong enough to stop buying unhealthy foods. If they are not available in the house the child can not snack on them.

If a child is use to having snacks everyday it is not a good idea to get rid of them all immediately. This will just increase the desire to want them, leading to tantrums and other negative behaviour. The idea is to reduce the bad foods and treats slowly. This will encourage the child to be more cooperative. Slowly introduce the child to healthy, less-fattening snacks instead. The aim is to finally get rid of them completely but over time.

Success at cutting down on the amount of snacks a child eats is more likely if the child feels involved. Parents could let their child clear the junk food from the home and help them to make a shopping list of healthy food to replace it. They could do the shop together, avoiding the sweet and crisp, cake and biscuit aisles. When parents are shopping with their children, they should check the labels together and decide whether the food is healthy or not. However, it is a good idea not to shop when hungry.

Parents may know which snacks are unhealthy, but all too often children are influenced by advertising and parents may succumb to their children's demands. Parents need to explain that unhealthy snacks are not good for them and how advertisements are ways for company to persuade people to buy things because they want to make money. It would be a good idea to take healthy alternatives out with them as an alternative. This will help wean them off the unhealthy food. Encourage children to 'listen to their tummies' and eat when they are hungry rather than out of habit.

Making fruits and vegetables available at home not only increases the children's consumption of these foods but also increases the adult's consumption of them too. The focus is on healthy food choices and eating right rather than counting calories. The ultimate aim is to ensure their children eat regular meals rather than graze on snack foods.

Tips for parents on how to provide a healthy, well-balanced diet and ideas to encourage a change in eating habits can be found on the BUPA website: www.bupa.co.uk.

Parental control

When parents provide early exposure to nutritious foods, such as fruit and vegetables, children like and eat more of such foods. However, it should be left to the child to decide how much they want to eat from what is offered. Parents should never force children to empty their plate.

Children can respond negatively to a parent's attempts to control them. They desire what they can't have. If a person tries to restrict what a child eats, even if they are doing it with good intentions, children will want the restricted foods more. This may be to the extent they become confused whether they want food because they are hungry, or because it is not allowed.

The child must want to change their situation. To do this they need to know what the situation is. It is important to explain why they are doing something rather than telling them they have to.

Teasing a child to make them want to change can have negative effects on self-esteem and may create psychological issues. Parents should never make negative comments about a child's weight not even as a joke.

Social eating

Parents should be aware of the social contexts in which foods are consumed because children develop preferences for food offered in positive situations. Parents should make an effort to make eating healthy foods a positive experience. They could do this by serving healthy foods at parties and other special events.

Parents can encourage healthy eating habits at home by increasing the number of family meals eaten together and by making sure healthy foods are served. Suggest they can make meal times fun by spending time talking to their children and discussing their days, or by playing word and memory games. Ensure the television is turned off and there are no distractions.

When eating together parents should encourage their child to chew food slowly and savour the taste. This will help the child to feel full and consequently they will be less likely to overeat at mealtimes. They could also encourage their child to be more involved in preparing the meal as this will make them more aware of what they are eating.

One of the main culprits indentified for the obesity epidemic is sugary drinks. It is a good idea to replace these water or sugar-free alternatives. Always have a jug of water available at the dinner table. Water helps flush toxins out of vital organs, carries nutrients to your cells and provides a moist environment for ear, nose and throat tissues. It aids concentration and if they are able to concentrate better they will achieve more.

Bullying

Being overweight as a child can cause psychological distress. Understanding the link between bullying and long-term psychological problems in children is important. When a child is overweight or obese, parents should understand that these boys and girls are at increased risk of being bullied. When a boy is overweight, parents need to be aware it is very common for them to become a bully. This is important to recognise because there are negative social outcomes for bullies too. They tend to grow up with difficulty forming adult relationships and also suffer from an increased risk of depression.

Recognising the signs of bullying in a child is an important step in breaking the chain of negative outcomes. Some signs to be aware of include; increased stress, depression, unexplained bruising, recurrent abdominal pain and vomiting, frequent or repeated accidents, hyperventilation, submissive behaviour and school refusal. If a parent has concerns about bullying they can seek advice from their child's school or if they wish a doctor / paediatrician.

Parents should be reassured that the school has an anti-bullying policy in place. Teachers should talk through the anti-bullying policy with the parents and re-assure them the matter is being taken seriously. An appointment should be made for the parent to discuss the matter further once the teacher has been able to investigate. Inform the parent you are going to interview the victim, the bully and anybody else who may have seen the incident and all the information will be passed on to the Headteacher, who will be kept informed at all stages.

If the matter can not be resolved by the class teacher the parent then knows they can approach the Headteacher who will be aware of what has occurred and what has been done so far by the teacher. Reassure the parent that the school will act promptly and firmly against all forms of bullying.

Raising self-esteem

Successful weight management improves self-esteem. Feeling confident in themselves can reduce the desire to turn to food for comfort. Parents can also help raise self-esteem by praising their child more often than they criticise them, because children's opinions of their self are influenced by the way their parents talk and act toward them. So, parents should show and tell their child they love and care for them and praise every success. By giving children, age-appropriate household responsibilities, they will also learn how to work with others by cooperating within the family.

Another idea to for parents to help raise their child's self-esteem is to make an inspirational poster. Use pictures from magazines to illustrate bold headings such as, 'You Can Do It', 'The Real You', 'Success' and 'I choose to eat healthy foods'. Encourage the child to make their posters look bold and interesting enough to inspire them. These headings can become daily affirmations and will help the child to realise anything is possible and will help them to focus on their goals and desires.

Undertaking activities together as a family will raise self-esteem. Parents could try growing their own vegetables with their children for fun, or arrange day trips.

Electronic devices

Over one quarter of today's youth are 'media multi-taskers' who go online to chat and play computer games, whilst watching TV, listening to music and using their mobile phone. Children spend more time sitting down using electronic devices than they do any other activity. This is more than likely a major cause of childhood obesity. The Government recommends parents should limit children's television viewing and other recreational screen time to less than two hours per day.

Using these electronic devices can lead to obesity by reducing children's physical activity and by encouraging poor eating habits, not only by exposing them to advertising for junk food, but often children eat in front of the television, or whilst playing the games. It is important for parents to be aware that many digital television stations do still show adverts for junk food as they do not have to follow the Government guidelines.

One way parents can help to reduce their child's weight is by not allowing their children to eat while watching television, or doing homework. Parents can also reduce the amount of time spent on electrical

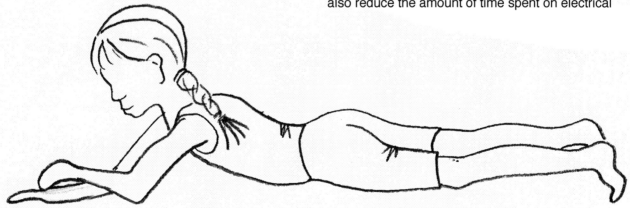

devices by removing them from the bedrooms and encouraging their child to be more physically active.

It is possible for parents to identify how much time is spent using electronic devices such as televisions, computers and hand-held games systems by having a family meeting to chart how much time is spent in these 'low-energy' activities and as a whole family they could discuss ways to replace this time with more physical activities.

Physical activity

According to the national diet and Nutrition Survey (2000), four out of ten boys and six out of ten girls do not do the minimum one hour a day of physical exercise recommended by the Government in 2007.

Physical activity gives people more energy to burn off excess fat. Keeping children active is the best way of preventing them becoming overweight. Parents should encourage their children to play outdoors because the more time children spend outdoors the higher their activity levels. It is understandable that many parents do not let their children play in the streets due to traffic and fear of strangers. But, there are many play areas and outside sports clubs that children can go to. Parents could go on walks and bike rides together, or go on family picnics to places where their children can be active and safe. Involve the child in the choice of activity. They will be more cooperative and it will encourage them to feel less scared of the long-term commitment to lose weight. The child will feel in control and valued.

A person always feels better after they have exercised even if they didn't want to do the exercise at first. Parents should encourage their children to persevere, as little things add up to big things. Support can take many forms from arranging access to after-school clubs, going to watch their children's activities or simply by playing with their children.

Sleep

Sleep is a highly active and complex state that is vital to our physical, mental and emotional health. A chronic lack of sleep diminishes the effectiveness of the body's immune system. People who have been deprived of sleep are slower and more prone to errors than those who have has a sufficient amount of sleep. It also has a significant impact on the way our bodies digest and process food. Primary aged children should get between ten and thirteen hours of sleep a night.

Improving a child's sleep habits and the quality of sleep can help with their weight management. This should include getting rid of nightlights and sleeping in an absolutely dark environment to increase their melatonin production. It is important to keep the eyes from registering light when they should be registering darkness. It is not a good idea to exercise before going to bed as a good workout can make you more alert, speed up your metabolism and energize you for the day ahead, but exercise right before bedtime can lead to a poor night's sleep. A calming bedtime ritual makes it easier for a child to relax, fall asleep and sleep through the night.

Pause for thought

Parents should be encouraged not to use the word 'diet' as it has negative implications. The children are not going on a diet but they are re-educating the way they think about food and activity.

It is important for parents to be aware how to contact the necessary specialist services that can help to deal with childhood obesity. At the end of Section Three is a sheet that parents or staff can fill in that contains spaces for them to make a note of named person and phone numbers / email addresses.

There is also a sample individual health plan that could be used within the school, for specific children, in the same way as an Individual Education Plan, or behaviour plan. Teachers can photocopy this sheet and complete in consultation with parents and there is one provided to complete with the child concerned. This will reinforce the child is ultimately in control and responsible for their own weight loss.

Charts, like the example below, are a good way to monitor the child's progress. The goal set at school

might be walk to school four out of five days, or bring a healthy lunchbox to school each day. Goals set at home could be, replace sugary drinks with water for four days of the week, or cycle for three days a week for twenty minutes. When they achieve the goal the day could be marked with a tick, sticker or smiley face. Once a week on an agreed day, the chart can be tallied to see if the weekly goal has been achieved.

Day	Mon	Tues	Wed	Thurs	Fri	Sat	Sun
Goal:							

Not achieving a goal can be detrimental to a child's self-esteem. If the child does not achieve their goal it is important they are not made to feel like a failure. If they did not manage it, the goal was too hard for them. Explain the parent should praise the child for trying and next time set an easier goal which is more attainable. Parents might also like to ask if there is anything they could do to help them achieve their target.

Class activities

There are 32 activities in Section Two, which provide a variety of ideas for healthy eating and physical activity. It is important that both healthy eating and physical exercise are taught alongside each other rather than splitting them up to emphasise it is important to consider both, particularly when trying to tackle obesity.

When undertaking the activities, remember at no point should you highlight anyone as being overweight or obese. The purpose of this book is to teach the children to understand the importance of healthy eating and doing regular exercise and have an opportunity to put these skills and their knowledge into practice. It is not meant to stigmatise anyone.

Food Pyramid

Learning Objective
To recognise there are many different types of food, which have different functions to help keep us healthy

Key Vocabulary
Carbohydrates, vitamins, protein, minerals, saturated fat, unsaturated fat, monounsaturated, polyunsaturated, dairy, fruit and vegetables

Organisation
Whole class discussion and individual work at the pupil's own level

Resources
- 'Food pyramid' activity sheet 1a (one enlarged copy)

- 'Food pyramid' activity sheet 1b (one per child)

- Scissors

- Glue

- Magazines and leaflets with pictures of fresh food from the five food groups

- Non-fiction books with pictures and information about food from the five food groups

Introduction
This activity looks at the five main food groups and how much should be eaten from each group to maintain a balanced diet. Discuss with the children what they already know about diet and introduce important vocabulary associated with healthy eating.

Explain:
- Carbohydrates are starchy foods that can be converted readily into glucose to provide energy to the body.

- Vitamins are essential substances that cannot be manufactured by the body, important for growth and development.

- Protein is used by our bodies to grow muscles, hair, nails, skin and internal organs. Diets rich in protein are often recommended for athletes and body builders. A good general rule of thumb for determining protein requirements would be one gram of protein for every kilogram (2.2 lbs.) of body weight. Too much protein can increase the risk of developing heart disease, stroke, kidney stones and osteoporosis.

- Minerals are necessary for building strong bones and teeth, controlling body fluids and turning the food we eat into energy. Essential minerals include: calcium, iron, magnesium, phosphorus, potassium, sodium and sulphur.

- Saturated fat raises the level of cholesterol in the blood, which can lead to coronary heart disease, liver problems and obesity. Obesity is a recognized disease. It has become a worldwide pandemic. Currently two-thirds of adults and a third of children are overweight or obese. The UK has the worst weight problem in Europe, with almost a quarter of adults classed as grossly overweight. Most worrying is the increase of obesity in children. Obesity rates have doubled among six-year-olds and trebled among 15-year-olds in the last ten years. Talk about some of the effects to health, motivation and self-esteem that obesity can cause, as outlined in chapter two.

- Unsaturated fat (monounsaturated or polyunsaturated) helps to improve cholesterol levels and prevent health risks. Unsaturated fat is essential to the proper functioning of the body. Fatty acids provide the raw materials that help to control blood pressure, blood clotting and many other functions. Stress that all fat is high in calories though, so people should limit their overall fat intake.

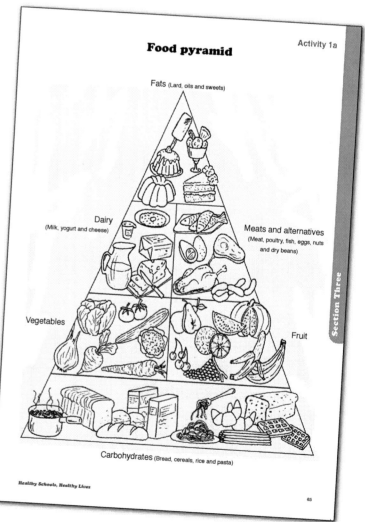

Food pyramid

Activity 1a

Fats (Lard, oils and sweets)

Dairy (Milk, yogurt and cheese)

Meats and alternatives (Meat, poultry, fish, eggs, nuts and dry beans)

Vegetables

Fruit

Carbohydrates (Bread, cereals, rice and pasta)

Healthy Schools, Healthy Lives

65

Section Two

Section Three

- Dairy foods are an important and easily absorbed source of calcium, which helps to keep teeth and bones strong and also provide the body with protein and vitamins A and B12.

- Fruit and Vegetables are a good source of many vitamins and minerals and should make up about one-third of the food eaten each day.

Main activity

Explain diet can affect the health of humans. A balanced diet is eating the correct amount of the right food types. A variety of food should be eaten from each food group every day to get the full range of carbohydrates, vitamins, minerals and proteins.

The illustration of the food pyramid on activity sheet 1a can be photocopied for use in the classroom or transferred to an overhead projector or interactive white board for use within the classroom. Explain what each food group is and what essential nutrients it provides the body with.

Tell the children we should eat more carbohydrates than anything else, which include bread, cereals, potatoes and other starchy food such as yams, pasta, rice, oats, noodles, maize and cornmeal. These foods are the main source of energy for the body and we should eat 6-11 portions a day.

Emphasise we should eat the fatty and sugary foods sparingly. This is the smallest group at the top of the pyramid. Saturated fats are not essential for a healthy balanced diet. Fats are organic compounds made up of carbon hydrogen and oxygen. They are the most concentrated source of energy in foods. In the west roughly 40% of calories come from fat. This needs to be reduced to 30%. Explain the difference between saturated fat and unsaturated fat.

A good visual demonstration to show the children the difference between the two types of fat is to let them compare a lump of solid lard to a liquid sunflower or olive oil. Explain how saturated fat is solid at room temperature whereas, unsaturated fat is liquid. Ask the children to think what this fat is doing to the inside of their body.

Allow adequate time for the children to complete the activity sheet by cutting and sticking the different food into the correct section.

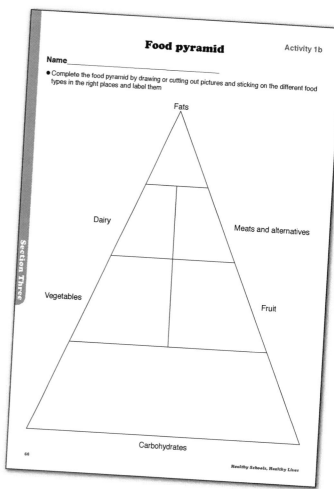

Plenary

Let the children show their completed activity sheets. Ask:
- Which food group should they eat the most from per day?

- Which food group should they eat the least from?

- How much fruit and vegetables should they aim to eat every day?

- What are the possible effects of eating too much fats and sugars?

Extension

Use non-fiction books to identify some foods that contain large amounts of fat such as crisps and chips and foods that contain excessive amounts of sugars, such as sweets and jams. The children could produce a display to show what they have found out about these foods.

Healthy or not

Learning Objective
To understand some food is good for us and some is not

Key Vocabulary
Healthy, unhealthy, meals, dinner, dessert, allergies, intolerances, famine

Organisation
Whole class discussion, group discussion and individual work at the pupil's own level.

Resources
● 'Healthy or not' activity sheet (one per group)

● Magazines, cookery books and leaflets with pictures of healthy and unhealthy dinners and desserts

● Non-fiction books about food allergies and intolerances

● Internet access

Introduction
Discuss what makes a healthy meal. Show pictures of the healthy and unhealthy dinners and desserts. The pictures on the activity sheet could be displayed on an overhead projector or interactive whiteboard for whole class discussion. Supplement this with pictures collected from cookery books, magazines and food leaflets.

Discuss with the children why they are healthy or why they are not healthy.

Main activity
Split the class into small groups and give each group a copy of the activity sheet 'Healthy or not'. Encourage the children to discuss which pictures they think are healthy and which ones are not.

Each group should only put a tick by the meals they think are healthy or a cross by the meals they think are unhealthy when the whole group has come to a consensus. The children from each group must justify their decisions.

Plenary
Ask if everyone has the same access to a healthy diet. Talk with the class about some of the Government initiatives, such as the school fruit and vegetable scheme outlined in chapter one.

Discuss that some people may have allergies or intolerances to different types of food and have to be careful what they eat. Consider world-wide issues such as, famine, religions and cultures.

Extension
Research what foods people can have allergies and intolerances to in library books and on the Internet. Provide time for these children to report their findings to the class.

What do we eat?

Activity 2

Name_____

● Put a tick by the foods you think are healthy and a cross by the ones you think are not healthy

Pie with chips	Spaghetti bolognaise
Fried breakfast	Fish, new potatoes and vegetables
Teacle sponge pudding	Fruit salad
Fruit jelly	Slice of chocolate cake

Healthy Schools, Healthy Lives

67

Section Two

Section Three

What do we eat?

Learning Objective
To examine their own diets and amount of physical activity they do and compare it to Government guidelines

Key Vocabulary
Diet, balanced, physical activity, exercise

Organisation
The 'What do we eat?' activity sheet should be given for homework at least a week before this lesson.

Class discussion and working with a partner

Resources
- What do we eat?' activity sheet (homework)

- 'Food pyramid' activity sheet 1a to use for analysis (one per pair)

- Access to a computer

Introduction
The 'What do we eat?' activity sheet has been designed for the children to do as homework to keep a record of what they eat over the week and then bring back to the classroom to decide whether they have eaten a healthy balanced diet.

There is also space to record how much exercise they have done and consider whether this was enough physical activity compared to the amount of food they have eaten and consider this against the Governments recommended daily activity of 60 minutes a day.

Explain the sheet to the children and that they need to record what they eat for their breakfast, lunch and dinner every day for a week. Point out there is a space to include snacks. Discuss how they can estimate how much exercise they do. Tell them walking to and from school counts.

Emphasise that you will be using the information they have collected in the classroom for a variety of different activities so it is important they bring the activity sheet back completed.

Main activity
Look at the information they have collected with a partner and compare the types of meals they have eaten.

Use what they have learnt about the food pyramid to explore if they have food from each food group in their diet. Write these questions on a whiteboard so all the children can see them to focus their discussion with their partner.
- Have they eaten the same everyday?

- Have they eaten the same as each other?

- What things are different?

- Over the week have they eaten a balanced and varied diet?

- Have could their diet be improved?

Plenary
Ask for volunteers to share what they have found out from their charts with the whole class.

Discuss general ideas on how diet can be improved:
- A healthy low-sugar cereal with milk and a piece of fruit is a good start to the day.

- Grill or bake instead of fry, steam instead of boil. Burgers, fish fingers and sausages are just as tasty when grilled, but have a lower fat content. Oven chips are lower in fat than fried chips.

-
- Fill up with fibre. Starchy foods which are rich in complex carbohydrates, such as potatoes, yams, pasta, rice and noodles are all filling and nutritious.

- Instead of snacks like chocolate, biscuits, cakes and crisps, choose healthy alternatives like fresh fruit, dried fruit or tinned fruit in natural juice, plain popcorn, crusty bread or crackers.

- Avoid fizzy drinks that are high in sugar. Substitute them with fresh juices diluted with water or sugar-free alternatives.

Extension
This activity could be adapted to form part of a daily diary that could be recorded on the computer as a healthy blog where the children document their fruit, vegetable and drink consumption and how many minutes of physical exercise they have each day.

Activity 3

What do we eat?

Name_____

Day	Monday	Tuesday	Wednesday	Thursday	Friday	Saturday	Sunday
Breakfast							
Lunch							
Dinner							
Snacks							
Exercise							

Section Two

Breakfast survey

Learning Objective
To consider what types of food make a healthy breakfast and which foods are not so good to eat in the morning.

Key Vocabulary
Breakfast, healthy, unhealthy, balanced, energy, fibre

Organisation
The 'Breakfast survey' activity sheet should be given for homework at least a week before this lesson

Whole class discussion, individual work at the pupil's own level and group discussion

Resources
● 'Breakfast survey' activity sheet

● A1 paper

● Marker pens

● Coloured pencils

● Rulers

Introduction
Ask the children to keep a breakfast diary of what they have eaten for breakfast each morning for a week. This could be completed for homework or done from memory in the classroom. Alternatively you could use the previously filled out, 'What do we eat?' activity sheet to obtain the raw data.

Stress that breakfast is the most important meal of the day because it gives you energy. Don't skip it! Research has shown that people who eat breakfast are often slimmer than those who skip breakfast as the energy it provides helps you burn more calories through the day.

Main activity
Ask the children to individually fill in the bar chart to show what they have eaten for breakfast over the seven days.

In small groups of about 5/6 children ask them to draw bar charts to show the different breakfast eaten by the children in their group over the seven days. This could be drafted out on large sheets of A1 paper and copied up neatly into their books.

Plenary
Answer questions about the data collated. What is the most popular breakfast? What is the healthiest breakfast? What is the least healthy breakfast and why? Encourage the children to give reasons for their answers. The bar charts and their findings can be displayed within the classroom.

Extension
Collate the information from everybody's activity sheets to make a whole class graph of what they eat for breakfast, which can be put on display.

Section Two

Breakfast survey

Name_____
● Keep a record of what you eat for breakfast over the week.

Monday _____

Tuesday _____

Wednesday _____

Thursday _____

Friday _____

Saturday _____

Sunday _____

● Draw a bar to show the different kinds of breakfasts you ate.

Amount eaten							
1							
2							
3							
4							
5							
6							
7							
NONE							

Type of breakfast eaten

● Which is the most popular breakfast? _____

● Was it a healthy option? Why?_____
_____
_____

● Why is it important to eat breakfast? _____
_____
_____

Healthy Schools, Healthy Lives

69

Section Three

Meals in a day

Learning Objective
To learn an adequate and varied diet is needed to keep healthy

Key Vocabulary
Breakfast, lunch, dinner, balanced, healthy, diet

Organisation
Whole class discussion, individual work on the activity sheet and paired consolidation work.

Resources
● 'Meals in a day' activity sheet (one per child)

● 'Food pyramid' activity sheet 1a (one enlarged)

● Paper plates (enough for one per child)

● Variety of medium such as textiles (including stuffing to produce 3D effects), papers, paints, chalks, coloured pencils and pastels.

Introduction
Remind children about the types of meals that are good for us and how we should try and obtain a balanced diet. Revisit the food pyramid and ask them to identify the five food groups.

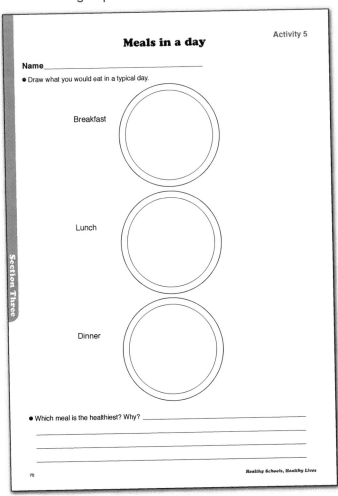

Main activity
Hand out the Meals in a day activity sheet. This activity sheet shows three plates for the children to draw their favourite meals on or if you wish, the meals they have recorded on one day of their chart. Ask the children to discuss in pairs, which one is the healthiest meal, the one they ate breakfast, lunch or dinner.

It is important to draw the children's attention to what they are eating even though they are not responsible for the meals that are served to them it is important they have an understanding and is essential grounding for making good food choices in the future. The children could make 3D collages of their food choices onto paper plates for display in the classroom.

Plenary
Ask the children to discuss in pairs if each meal is balanced. Do they achieve a balance over the whole day? How could they improve the meals they eat? Stress variety and balance are key to a good meal.

Extension
Get them to label their plates to show which food group the different food items are from.

Healthy eating

Learning Objective
To record ideas about foods using drawings and charts

Key Vocabulary
Sort, healthy, unhealthy, columns,

Organisation
Whole group discussion and small groups of 4/5 children

Resources
- Large sheets A1 paper

- Marker pens

- Small whiteboards (enough for one each)

- Large class whiteboard

- 'Healthy eating' activity sheet (one per child for recording their choices)

Introduction
Write the list of foods onto large sheets of paper to show the class. Try to think of ideas not on the activity sheet. Hold each one up and ask whether they think it is healthy or not. Divide the whiteboard into two columns and ask for volunteers to come up and stick the meal in the right column. Children can vote by writing healthy or unhealthy on small whiteboards and holding them up.

Main activity
Look at the list of foods on the healthy eating activity sheet. Use the large sheets of A1 paper to draw their own chart. In small groups they should discuss the reasons why they think the foods are healthy and place them in the correct column. The food item can not be placed in a column until the entire group are in agreement on whether it is healthy or not. Copy their decisions onto their activity sheet as a record of what they have done.

Plenary
Ask for a spokesperson from each group to say where they have placed the food type and why? Encourage the children to give reasons for their choices.

Extension
Add their own ideas for healthy and unhealthy food to the columns to demonstrate an understanding of what is healthy for them to eat and what is not.

Section One

Healthy eating

Activity 6

Name_____

- Look at the list of foods below:

banana   kidney beans   ice cream

sweets   leeks   chips   crisps   salmon

chocolate   cheese   fish fingers   sausages

sticky toffee pudding   yogurt   chicken and mushroom pie

milk   burgers   plums   pizza

tin tomatoes   jelly   new potatoes   dumplings

lamb chops   carrots

- Which are healthy and which are not healthy? Put them in the correct column on the table.

Healthy	Not healthy
Why are these healthy foods?	Why are these unhealthy foods?

Healthy Schools, Healthy Lives   71

Section Three

A healthy balanced meal

Learning Objective
To make an informed judgement on what can be classified as a healthy meal

Key Vocabulary
Fat, saturated, unsaturated, monounsaturated, polyunsaturated

Organisation
Whole class discussion and individual work at the pupil's own level

Resources
● Packaging of a range of ready meals for main courses and desserts

● 'A healthy balanced meal' activity sheet 7a or 7b (one per child, which sheet you decide to use is dependent on child's needs)

● Coloured pencils

Introduction
Hold up the different packaging for the pre-packed foods which you have available. Discuss which type of ready-meal might contain the most fat and why they think this. Consider the ingredients that have gone into making the variety of meals. List them on the whiteboard or show enlargements on an interactive whiteboard.

Some ideas for pre-prepared meals to try and collect are:
● Curry sauces

● Enchiladas

● Lasagne

● Pasta dishes

● Quarter pounder

● Steak and kidney pie

Tell the children, according to the British Nutrition Foundation most of these meals are so fatty they should only be eaten once a week.

Explain there is a risk of not recognising how much fat there is in some pre-packaged foods, which can lead to obesity. Reinforce the idea that it is better to cook their own meals to ensure only healthy and non-fattening ingredients are used.

Main activity
Draw a healthy balanced meal on the plate and explain why it is healthy. Label the food and name which food group it is from. There are two choices of sheet available the empty plate or the plate showing the portion size of the different food types for a balanced diet. 'A healthy balanced meal' activity sheet 7b could be enlarged onto an interactive white board or over head projector to give the class a visual impression of the portion sizes.

Plenary
Ask which food type should we eat the most of? Which food type should we eat the least of?

Extension
Take a look at pre-packaged dessert packaging. Point out the sugar content in these foods. Try and get a range of low-fat foods to look at as well, such as normal and low-fat digestive biscuits and observe the sugar content in them. Explain that many low-fat foods may have lower saturated fat but do tend to have higher sugar content. Point out too much sugar is just as bad for you as too much fat.

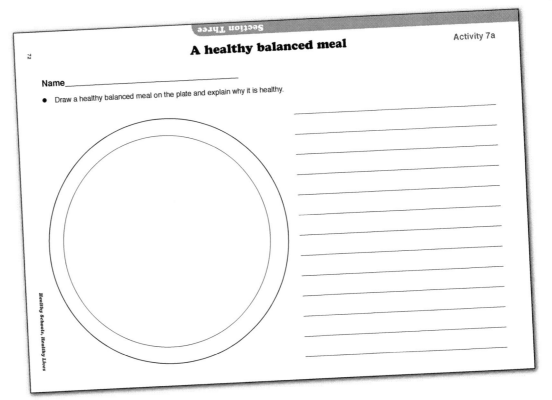

Section Three

A healthy balanced meal

Activity 7a

Name_____

● Draw a healthy balanced meal on the plate and explain why it is healthy.

A rainbow of food

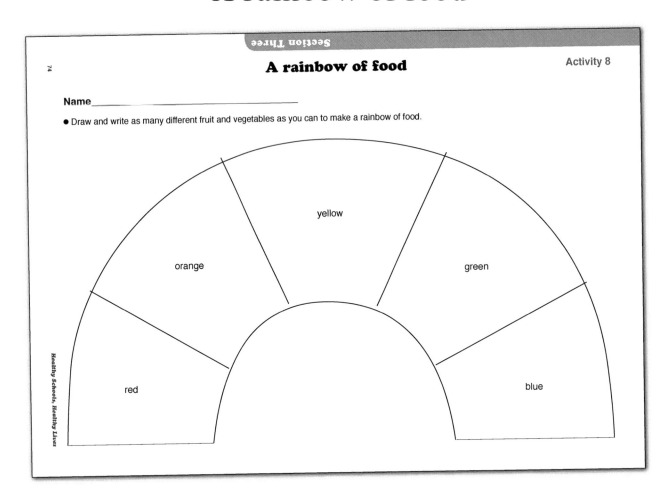

Section Three

74

A rainbow of food

Activity 8

Name_____

● Draw and write as many different fruit and vegetables as you can to make a rainbow of food.

orange

yellow

green

red

blue

Healthy Schools, Healthy Lives

Learning Objective
To recognise there is a wide range of fruit and vegetables to choose from.

Key Vocabulary
The names of a wide variety of fruit and vegetables, including some they may not have heard of before

Organisation
Whole class discussion and individual work

Resources
● Art paper

● Range of art resources, such as textiles (including stuffing to produce 3D effects), papers, paints, chalks, coloured pencils and pastels.

● 'A rainbow of food' activity sheet (one per child)

● Magazines and leaflets with pictures of fresh fruit and vegetables to cut up

● Scissors

● Glue

● Information books on fruit and vegetables

Introduction
Bring in fresh, or collect pictures of, fruit and vegetables and ask the children to name them. Include less well-known examples such as Sharon fruit, kiwi, artichoke and okra.

Main activity
Draw and write as many different fruits and vegetables to make a rainbow of fruit and vegetables. This idea could be used for a large wall display within the classroom. You could also use magazines to cut out pictures of fruit and vegetables, or get the children to draw and decorate fruit and vegetables using a variety of mediums. Ask the children to label the fruit and vegetables.

Plenary
Have they discovered any fruit and vegetables they did not previously know about?

Extension
They could make a fruit and vegetable encyclopaedia, with information on what country the fruit or vegetable originated from and some ideas of what they could be used for. Tell the children how some fruits and vegetables are not only used in cooking, but as remedies when people feel unwell and for dyeing clothes. Can they find a fruit or vegetable for every letter of the alphabet?

Section Two

Fruit and vegetables around the world

Learning Objective
To gain an understanding that different types of fruit and vegetables are grown all over the world

Key Vocabulary
Names of popular types of fruit and vegetables, import, export

Organisation
Small groups of 4/5 children

Resources
● Atlases, globes, Google Earth and maps of the world

● Enlarged 'Fruit and vegetables around the world' activity sheet (one per group)

● Non-fiction books about fruits and vegetables

● Internet access

Introduction
Tell the children they are going to investigate fruit and vegetables from other countries. Find out where some of the more popular fresh fruit and vegetables come from like bananas, mangos, pineapples, peppers and carrots, green beans and sweetcorn. Which ones are from the UK? Which ones are imported? Talk about the weather conditions needed for different types of fruit and vegetables to grow.

Make two lists on the whiteboard of 'Fruit and vegetables mostly grown in the UK' and 'Fruit and vegetables mostly grown abroad', so the children can refer to it during the lesson.

Main activity
In small groups the children can investigate what countries the fruits and vegetables are from. Draw the fruits and vegetables on the enlarged copy of the world map on the 'Fruit and vegetables around the world' activity sheet.

Explain some of the fruits and vegetables may be imported from more than one country. Give them time to look the fruit and vegetables up on the Internet to find out more information about them.

Plenary
Discuss how fruit and vegetables grown in the UK are exported to other countries. What transport could be used? Why do we export and import fruits and vegetables?

Extension
Ask the children to think of problems in transporting food over long distances such as it might rot. Discuss how such problems could be reduced.

Section Two

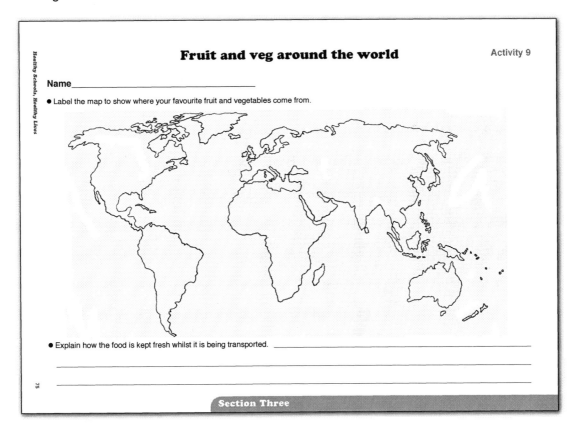

Fruit and veg around the world Activity 9

Healthy Schools, Healthy Lives

Name_____

● Label the map to show where your favourite fruit and vegetables come from.

● Explain how the food is kept fresh whilst it is being transported. _____

_____

75

Section Three

Fruit and Vegetable Tasting

Learning Objective
To experience different types of fruits and vegetables that they may not have had the pleasure of experiencing before

Key Vocabulary
Names of the chosen fruits and vegetables to taste in the classroom, like, dislike, taste, texture

Organisation
Small groups of four or five children

Resources
- Variety of fruits and vegetables suitable for tasting

- Paper plates (enough for one per group)

- 'Fruit and Vegetable Tasting' activity sheet (one per child as a record of the fruit and vegetables they liked)

- Sharp knife

- Peeler

- Corer

- Clingfilm

Introduction
Explain we need to eat at least five different fruits and vegetables a day. Fruit and vegetables help with digestion and contain essential nutrients to help keep the body healthy. Different forms of fruit and vegetables such as fresh, tinned, 100% juice or smoothie, dried and frozen, all count towards the five a day target.

Most packaging now contains a five-a-day label, which shows how many portions of fruit and vegetables a typical serving of the food contains. Explain that a rough guide to a portion is about a handful. But, it is important to note that juices and pulses only count as one portion no matter how much you eat or drink in a day.

Main activity
Have a selection of fruit and vegetables available to taste. Try to get a few they may not recognise or have tasted before such as olives or dragon fruit. Do not forget to send out permission slips before attempting any tasting activities in the classroom and check if any of the children have any food allergies or intolerances.

Split the class into small groups and put enough fruit and vegetable onto the paper plates for each group to try a small piece of each. The fruit and vegetable should be prepared before the lesson and the plate covered with Clingfilm until required. Have some uncut fruit to show the class what it looks like whole. Do not forget to ask the children to wash their hands before touching the fruit and vegetables.

Encourage the children to talk about the fruit and vegetables. What does it look like? Is it hard, soft, juicy or crunchy? Can you eat the skin / peel?

Each child should record the fruit and vegetables they tasted in two columns: 'like' and 'dislike'. Encourage the children to add any others they know they like or dislike to the chart on the activity sheet.

Plenary
Discuss which fruit and vegetables they liked best. Ask them to describe what each one tasted like.

Extension
Make a bar chart of the classes favourite fruits and vegetables.

Fruit and vegetable tasting — Activity 10

Name _____
- Taste a selection of different fruit and vegetables
- Complete the chart

Like	Dislike

- Add any other fruit and vegetables you know you like to the chart.
- What are your top five favourite fruits: _____
- What are your top five favourite vegetables: _____

76

Healthy Schools, Healthy Lives

Five a day

Section Two

Eat your 5 a day

Activity 11

Name_____

● Design and make a poster to persuade people to eat five different fruits and vegetables a day

Healthy Schools, Healthy Lives

77

Section Three

Introduction

Brainstorm some of the pros and cons of trying to eat five different types of vegetables a day. For example, they are good for you as they provide vitamins, minerals and fibre, which helps to improve concentration and will help to reduce risk of disease. It is important to acknowledge they may not be as easy to prepare as pre-packaged food, they can sometimes be perceived as more expensive and probably the most important fact is their parents may not buy fruit and vegetables.

Brainstorm some good, catchy captions for their posters that they could use in their persuasive posters to try and persuade people to eat five different fruit and vegetables a day, such as, 'Five a day helps you work rest and play'. List the children's ideas so they can refer to them.

Main activity

Design a poster to persuade people to eat five different fruits and vegetables a day. Think of ways they could increase their daily intake of fruit and vegetables. Suggest they could eat an apple or banana at lunch or for breakfast, have a smoothie or add raisins to their cereal. The posters can be displayed around the class and the school.

Plenary

Ask the children to show their posters and explain the reasoning behind the message they are trying to convey.

Extension

Make a more detailed leaflet or pamphlet to explain how fruit and vegetables are good for you.

Learning Objective

To recognise five portions of fruit and vegetables should be eaten every day.

Key Vocabulary

Concentration, disease, caption, catchphrase, vitamins, energy, persuade

Organisation

Whole class and individual work

Resources

● 'Five a day' activity sheet (one per child)

● A4 paper for leaflets

Design a smoothie

Learning Objective
To recognise healthy food can be fun.

Key Vocabulary
Smoothie, names of fruits used such as orange, pineapple, apple, pear, banana, mango, liquidiser, allergy, hygiene

Organisation
Send out letters with returnable permission slip to check if children have any allergies, intolerances or food that must be avoided on religious grounds a few days before this activity takes place.

Work with partners

Resources
- 'Design a smoothie' activity sheet (one per child as a record)
- Selection of fruit pre-cut
- Sharp knife
- Peeler
- Corer
- Paper plates
- Plastic cups
- Liquidiser

Introduction
Explain to the children they are going to design a healthy smoothie. Do they know what goes in a smoothie? Explain a smoothie is made of 100% fruit and no other added ingredients. Brainstorm ideas of fruit they might use to make smoothie.

Which fruit might contain a lot of juice? Which fruits would give the smoothie a thicker consistency? Show the class what fruit there is available to choose from for their smoothies. Ensure there is a large and varied selection.

Main activity
In pairs ask the children to write down their smoothie recipes and encourage the children to give them exotic names, like 'Strawberry Sensation' or 'Mango Fandango'.

Make the smoothies and have group tasting sessions. Do not forget to send out permission slips before attempting any tasting activities in the classroom and check if any of the children have any allergies. Remember when using food good hygiene should be shown at all times. They should wash their hands, wear aprons and tie back long hair. Reinforce correct use of the kitchen equipment such as, knives and liquidisers.

Try to pre-cut the fruit into even chunks before the session starts. This will help to divide it fairly amongst the groups.

Plenary
Afterwards they could judge each smoothie according to taste and texture. Ask if they liked their smoothie? What did they like most about their smoothie? What didn't they like about their smoothie? What would they change?

Children could vote for their favourite smoothie and the recipes could be shared.

Extension
Write an improved smoothie recipe after tasting their original design.

Drink 8 glasses

Learning Objective
To learn that water is just as important to staying healthy as solid food.

Key Vocabulary
Water, healthy, fluid, climate, dehydration, rehydration, toxins, replenish

Organisation
Class discussion and individual work

Resources
- 'Drink 8 glasses' activity sheet (one per child)
- Internet access
- Magazines with pictures of safe drinking water sources
- Scissors
- Glue
- A4 paper

Introduction
Explain how much water a person needs to drink, depends on their health, how active they are and whether they are in a hot or a cold country. No single formula will fit everyone, but knowing more about the body's need for fluids will help to estimate how much water to drink each day.

Water is about 60 percent of your body weight. Every system in your body depends on water. It flushes toxins out of vital organs, carries nutrients to your cells and provides a moist environment for ear, nose and throat tissues.

Lack of water can lead to dehydration, a condition that occurs when you don't have enough water in your body to carry out normal functions. However, too much water can affect the balance of salts in the body causing "water intoxication", which also can be fatal.

In climates such as the UK, we should drink approximately 1.2 litres (6 to 8 glasses) of fluid every day to stop us getting dehydrated. In hotter climates the body needs more than this. We also get some fluid from the food we eat.

Every day we lose water through breathing, perspiration, urine and bowel movements. For the body to function properly, we must replenish its water supply by consuming beverages and foods that contain water.

Explain water is treated to make it safe to drink. Tell the class drinking water from an unknown source is unsafe.

Main activity
The message to get across is that we should be drinking approximately eight glasses of water a day. Tell the class they are going to design a poster to remind people to drink enough water every day. Explain the importance of drinking enough fluids and how it helps aid concentration and if they are able to concentrate better they will achieve more in class.

They should colour in the glasses at the bottom of the activity sheet to show how much they have drunk so far that day. Explain one glass is equal to about 250ml so they are aiming to drink about two litres a day.

Plenary
Explain that for their homework they are going to write down everything they drink for one week. They should try to put down how much they drink (a glass, a can, a mug) as well as what they drink.

Tell them providing drinking water in schools help pupils and teachers concentrate. Drinking tap water reduces transport costs and will in turn help to tackle climate change.

Extension
Ask the children to list or draw all the ways they use water in their daily lives. Then get the children to think about all the different sources of water. Get them to create their own water book, using pictures they have drawn, found in magazines or on the Internet.

Create a display entitled: 'Water is precious'. Discuss how water is cleaned and how some people around the world do not have clean water like we do in the UK.

A healthy sandwich

Learning Objective
To demonstrate an understanding of healthy ingredients

Key Vocabulary
Sandwich, healthy, healthier, healthiest, balanced, hygiene,

Organisation
Permission slips for tasting activity, checking for food allergies and religious abstention should be collected in a few days in advance of the lesson.

Whole class discussion and working with a partner.

Resources
- Food pyramid 1a activity sheet (one enlarged)

- 'A healthy sandwich' activity sheet (one per child as a record)

- Knives

- Chopping boards,

- Selection of breads white, wholemeal, rolls, pita, wraps, fajitas, etc.

- Selection of spreads, such as margarine, mayonnaise, humous, salad cream, tomato sauce, etc.

- Selection of fillings, such as lettuce, tomato, cucumber, tuna, ham, pickle, etc.

Introduction
Explain to the children they are going to design a healthy sandwich. Do they know how to make a sandwich? Brainstorm ideas of the things they like to put in their sandwiches and whether these are healthy or not. Use an enlarged version of the 'Food pyramid' activity sheet 1a to reinforce the types of foods they need to eat to have a balanced diet.

Main activity
Encourage the children to look at the five food groups and choose something from each group to make their sandwich healthy and balanced. Which foods might they need more of? Which foods will they need to use sparingly?

Explain they can use different types of bread, such as rolls, pita bread, tortilla wraps, fajitas, etc. Ask them to consider healthy fillings and good combinations of healthy fillings. Again refer to the diagram of the food pyramid to help them consider their options.

Get the children to write down their sandwich recipes and encourage the children to give their sandwiches a name, such as the BLT.

Allow time for the children to make their sandwiches and have group tasting sessions. Do not forget to send out permission slips before attempting any tasting activities in the classroom and checking if any of the children have any allergies. Remember when using food good hygiene should be shown at all times. They should wash their hands, wear aprons and tie back long hair. Reinforce correct use of the kitchen equipment such as, knives and chopping boards.

Plenary
Afterwards they could judge their sandwiches according to taste and whether it achieved the goal of being healthy. Ask did they like their sandwich? What did they like most about their sandwich? What didn't they like about their sandwich? Could they have made them healthier?

Extension
Children could vote for their favourite sandwich and the recipes could be shared. Which sandwich was the healthiest? Why? Suggest the children could use these ideas in their lunch boxes.

Section Two

Section Three

Healthy sandwich
Activity 14

Name_____
- Design a healthy balanced sandwich.

Carbohydrates	Dairy	Protein	Fruit and Veg	Fats and sugars

- Name your sandwich _____

- How did you make your sandwich? _____

- What did you like most about your sandwich? _____

- What would you change? _____

80

Healthy Schools, Healthy Lives

Healthy lunchbox

Learning Objective
To demonstrate an understanding of a healthy balanced meal

Key Vocabulary
Lunchbox, healthy, balanced, carbohydrates, vitamins, protein, dairy, fruit, vegetable

Organisation
Class discussion and individual work at the child's own level

Resources
● 'Healthy lunchbox' activity sheet (one per child)

Introduction
Explain to the children they are going to design a healthy lunchbox. They should keep the lunchbox balanced by ensuring there is a range of food from the different food groups. Discuss what should go in a lunchbox. List their ideas on the whiteboard. Remind the children they all need to pack a drink. What sorts of drinks would help them to concentrate in school?

Discuss how high sugar foods can cause some children to become hyperactive and unable to concentrate, or for some people it can have the opposite effect and make them feel drowsy and unable to concentrate. Remind the children that the items in their lunchbox should be able to be consumed during the time allocated for school lunch.

Main activity
Use their healthy sandwich idea. Remember to pack a drink and remember to try and get something from the four main food groups. Remind children that sweets and fizzy drinks are not permitted in school as they are not healthy.

Plenary
Ask for volunteers to share their ideas for their healthy lunchbox. Do the rest of the class agree?

Extension
Make a list of things that it would NOT be a good idea to include and explain why these should not be taken for school lunch.

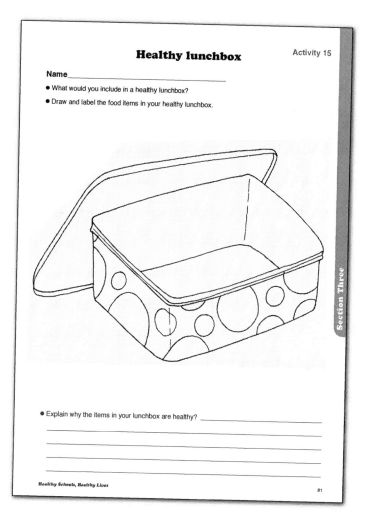

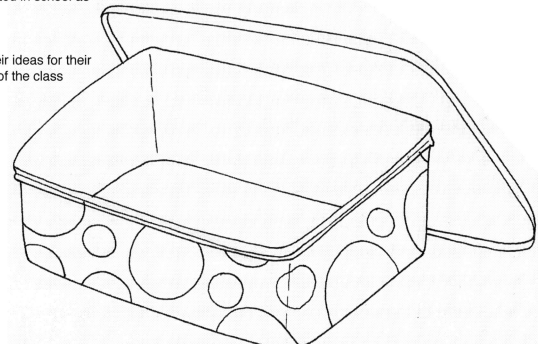

Section Two

Portion control

Learning Objective
To recognise what sensible servings look like

Key Vocabulary
Portion, serving, control, sensible, calories, overeating, mindful eating

Organisation
Whole class discussion and working with a partner

Resources
- 'Portion control' activity sheet 16a (one per pair)
- Multi-link
- Sand
- Water
- Pebbles
- Paper
- Scissors
- Plastic cups
- Plates
- Teaspoons
- Deck of cards
- CD
- Cassette tape box
- Large egg
- Tennis ball
- Paper pre-cut to the size of a chequebook
- 'Portion distortion' activity sheet 16b

Introduction
Food labels contain how much is recommended per serving. It is important to look carefully at the labels because sometimes the packet may be for two or more servings. By eating the whole pack people could be eating twice as much as they should. If we eat less, we consume fewer calories. If we do not eat enough food we will not have the energy to burn off the fat. This is why eating sensible portions is important.

Main activity
Explain to the class they are going to measure the suggested food portions on the activity sheet and compare them to standard serving sizes from Nutrition Facts labels on packaging. As food items are not readily available it is possible to improvise using other items such as multilink, sand, water and pebbles, etc. ask the children to use the activity sheet to physically make the right size portion of food and present it on a plate. In this way they can see for themselves how big a portion size is. Discuss whether this is bigger of smaller than they thought.

Plenary
Explain controlling portions is key to weight control and 'mindful eating' is a way to help master portion control.

Everybody needs to:
- Think about what and how much they are eating.
- Eat slowly, taste each bite.
- Recognise how often they are eating.

By 'mindful eating', we can monitor our choices and give our bodies the chance to respond to what we consume. This way we can enjoy food and share the cooking and dining experience with others, while recognising when we have eaten enough so that we don't overeat. We all need to train our bodies, eyes, and heads to recognise what sensible servings look like.

Extension
Ask the children to have a go at the 'Portion distortion' activity sheet 17b. Point out the calories and amount of exercise required to burn off the calories are approximate but the activity sheet does give an idea of how portion sizes have increased today compared to twenty-five years ago.

A burger today has 600 calories which is twice the amount of calories as 25 years ago and would take about 1hour, 30 minutes to burn doing exercise such as casual walking. The bottle of drink would contain approximately 340 calories and take about an hour to burn off. The muffin would be about 600 calories and the popcorn around 750 calories which would take approximately two hours to burn off.

Activity sheet 16a

Portion size   Activity 16a

Name_____

Food type	Portion of ...	Size	
Carbohydrates (6-11 servings a day)	Cereal	fist	
	Pancake	CD	
	Pasta/rice/potato	tennis ball	
	Bread	cassette tape case	
Fruit and vegetables (5 a day)	Salad	tennis ball	
	Fruit	tennis ball	
	Vegetables	tennis ball	
	Raisins	Large egg	
Dairy (2-3 servings a day)	Cheese	small matchbox	
	Ice-cream	tennis ball	
	Milk	fist	
	Yogurt	fist	
Meat and alternatives (2-4 servings a day)	Meat/poultry	deck of cards	
	Grilled fish	chequebook	
	Dried beans	large egg	
Fats (Use sparingly)	Oil	teaspoon	
	Jam	teaspoon	

82

Healthy Schools, Healthy Lives

Section Two

Section Three

Plaque attack

Learning Objective
To emphasise the need to establish good dental habits early in life, for life

Key Vocabulary
Teeth, hygiene, sugar, plaque, tooth decay, dentist, Fluoride, rot

Organisation
Whole class discussion and individual work at the child's own level

Resources
● Models of teeth, real teeth

● Small mirrors for examining own teeth

● 1 bottle of Fluoride mouthwash

● 2 eggs

● 1 bottle of vinegar

● 3 transparent plastic cups

Introduction
Explain to the class that sugar left in the mouth is eaten by bacteria. The bacteria uses sugar as a form of energy to make acid that rots teeth and causes tooth decay.

Taking care of our teeth prevents tooth decay. We can take care of our teeth by:
● brushing twice a day – morning and night

● eating the right foods (not too many sugary ones)

● visiting the dentist regularly

Many snacks and drinks we consume contain sugar. Each time you eat a snack containing sugar or starch (carbohydrates), the resulting acid attack on your teeth can last up to 20 minutes. A single can of fizzy drink contains up to 10 teaspoons of sugar, and natural sugar in apples or other fruit can also rot your teeth if you do not look after them properly. Foods that are eaten during a meal are not as harmful because of the additional saliva produced whilst eating a meal. Saliva helps to wash food particles from the mouth and reduces the damage from acid. Sugary foods help the bacteria multiply faster and forms plaque.

Dairy foods, such as yogurt, cheese, milk and milk products contain calcium, which is an essential nutrient for the development of bones and teeth and helps fight against plaque.

Main activity
Emphasise it is very important to brush our teeth regularly. Tell the class we are going to do an experiment to show how sugar may decay teeth and how brushing teeth with a fluoride toothpaste can help prevent tooth decay.

Pour four inches of the Fluoride mouthwash into one of the plastic cups and then place an egg in the solution. Ensure it is totally covered. Let it sit for about five minutes. Remove the egg. Pour four inches of vinegar into each of the remaining two containers. Put the egg that has been treated with the Fluoride into one container of vinegar and the untreated egg in the other container of vinegar.

Let the children observe how one egg starts to bubble as the vinegar (an acid) starts to attack the minerals in the egg shell.

Plenary
Ask why they think the untreated egg is bubbling and the one that was coated in mouthwash is not? How do they think the Fluoride has protected the teeth? Explain there is Fluoride in toothpaste and this helps protect the teeth in the same way.

Extension
Children can make a list of foods they think are bad for teeth. Tell them how fruit contains acids and sugars that can rot the teeth in the same way as sweets.

Plaque attack Activity 17

Name_____
● What were we testing?_____

● What did we do?_____

● What did you observe?

● What does this mean for your teeth?_____

84 *Healthy Schools, Healthy Lives*

Section Two

Section Three

Dental health

Learning Objective
To emphasise what we eat effects our teeth as well as our weight

Key Vocabulary
Teeth, hygiene, molars, premolars, canine, incisors, brushing, plaque, tooth decay

Organisation
Letter home before the session to explain the children will be using disclosing tablets and asking for their toothbrushes and toothpaste to be bought in to school

Whole class discussion and working with a partner

Resources
● Dental health activity sheet (one per child)

● Disclosing tablets
(one per child – check instructions)

● Children's own toothbrushes and toothpaste

● Plastic mirrors

● Plastic cups

● Drinking water

● Timers / stop watches

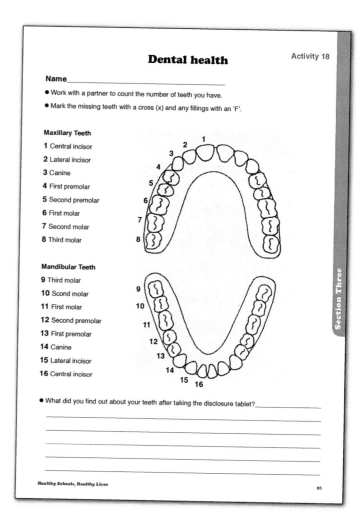

Introduction
Hand out the mirrors and give the children adequate time to look at their teeth. Use the activity sheet to explain the names of the different type of teeth and see if they can identify them in their own mouths and their partners. Record their observations on the activity sheet.

Main activity
Discuss the cleanliness of their mouths. Ask how they keep their teeth clean. Ask what will happen if they do not keep their teeth clean. Remind children that fluoride in toothpaste helps to prevent tooth decay and protects teeth from the harmful effects of plaque. Working in pairs, one person brushes their teeth before taking the disclosing tablet and the other does not brush their teeth.

The child not brushing their teeth should time their partner brushing their teeth for two minutes. Both chew a disclosing tablet. The children should look at the amount of stains on the brushed teeth compared to the teeth that were not brushed. What do they notice?

Plenary
Discuss why even after brushing some teeth were still stained by the disclosing tablet. Emphasise that it is important to brush teeth correctly so no areas of

plaque are missed. Explain the plaque and the stains can be removed by brushing correctly. Allow time for the children to brush away all the stains from their teeth. This can also be timed to show how long it takes to brush their teeth correctly. Tell the children to help reduce tooth decay they should eat a sensible, balanced diet and avoid frequent snacking between meals. They should also clean their teeth carefully at least twice a day.

Extension
Children can make a poster to reinforce the message on how to reduce tooth decay. This could also include regular check ups with the dentist and using a fluoride toothpaste, brushing correctly and flossing.

Section Two

Nutritional facts

Section Three

Nutritional facts

Activity 19

Name_____

● Look at the nutritional values on the wrappers of different foods. Complete the table.

Items	Calories	Sugar	Fats	Saturates	Salt	Healthy	Reason why?

● Tick the items you think are healthy

● Write the reasons you think these items are healthy or why you think they are not healthy.

Healthy Schools, Healthy Lives

Learning Objective
To recognise and understand nutritional food values

Key Vocabulary
Protein, fat, carbohydrate, fibre, vitamin, mineral, fluid

Organisation
Small groups of about 4/5 children

Resources
● 'Nutritional facts' Activity sheet (one per group)

● Clean food and drink labels showing nutritional facts from a variety of foods, including tinned, packets and fresh food types.

● A1 paper

● Marker pens

Introduction
Tell the class it is a legal requirement for food labels to include ingredient lists and a nutritional table. The ingredients must be listed in descending order of quantity. Explain the 'Per 100g' column is more useful for comparing foods than the 'per serving' column, as a serving could be different amounts. Remind the class that the five a day logo shows how many portions of fruit and vegetables a typical serving of the food contains.

Main activity
Ask the children to look at the nutritional values of different foods and identify the amount of calories, sugar, fat, saturates and salt they contain. Ensure each group has a variety of food types to investigate and use the information they find to complete the chart on the 'Nutritional facts' activity sheet. Which is the healthiest? Which is the least healthy? Why?

Tell the children they should be aware of added sugar in drinks, cereal bars, yoghurts and ready-made meals. Ask the children to think about what would happen if some of the information was missing; for example, 'Best before' or 'Use by' dates.

Plenary
Ask each group to make up a quiz of five questions based on the label information they have recorded on their chart. Use large sheets of A1 paper and marker pens. One person in the group could scribe. Ask the groups to swap quizzes and charts to answer each others questions.

Extension
Discuss why it is important for some people with allergies to read labels carefully.

Traffic lights

Learning Objective
To recognise and use the food traffic light system to make healthy food choices

Key Vocabulary
Traffic light system, healthy, nutritional, nutrition, red, amber, green

Organisation
Individual work

Resources
- 'Traffic light' activity sheet (one per child)

- Clean food and drink labels showing nutritional facts some with and some without traffic light labelling if possible

Introduction
Explain the traffic light labelling on food packaging. Discuss how it makes it easier for people to make healthy food choices. Tell the class food products with traffic light labels on the front of the pack show at-a-glance if the food has high, medium or low amounts of fat, saturated fat, sugars and salt. This helps to get a better balance.

If there is a red light on the front of the pack, the food is high in something we should be trying to cut down on. If it is amber, this is alright but people should aim to go for green for that nutrient some of the time too. Green means the food is low in these unhealthy nutrients. The more green lights, the healthier the choice.

Many of the foods with traffic light colours will have a mixture of red, amber and greens highlighted. People should aim to choose more greens and ambers, and fewer reds to ensure a healthy diet. Some of the labels look slightly different but the meaning is the same.

The traffic light colours make it easier for people to compare products at-a-glance. The label also tells you how much of each nutrient is in a portion. If two labels have similar colours people can compare these figures, and choose the one that is lower to make a healthier choice.

Main activity
Look at a variety of food packaging and decide what its overall value should be according to the traffic light labelling. Is there more red, amber or green lights? Place the food in the correct place on the activity sheet. If the food packaging does not use the traffic light system ask the children to make a judgement based on the saturated fat, salt and sugar content of each particular food.

Plenary
Ask the children to look next time they are at the supermarket and see what types of food have the traffic light labelling. The Food Standards Agency recommends that traffic light colours are used on processed convenience foods such as ready meals, pizzas, sausages, burgers, pies, sandwiches and breakfast cereals.

Extension
Look at the ingredients lists on the food packaging and ask the children to identify what the food contains most of. Remind the children that the ingredients must be listed in descending order of quantity.

Traffic lights

Activity 20

Name_____
- Classify the different foods according to the traffic light system.
- Give reasons for your choices

Red

I think these foods are red because…

Amber

I think these foods are amber because…

Green

I think these foods are green because…

Healthy Schools, Healthy Lives

87

Learning Objective
To use their knowledge of healthy foods to design their own healthy menus

Key Vocabulary
Menu, starter, main course, dessert,

Organisation
Work with a partner and individual work at the child's own level

Resources
- 'Healthy menu' activity sheet (one per child)

- School menus (enough for at least one per pair)

- Selection of menus from restaurants. These can be found on the internet

Introduction
Explain to the children they are going to design a healthy menu. Their menu should be balanced. Examine the school hot lunch menu and discuss the options. Look at what is available to eat over the day, week and term.

How have the caterers ensured that the menu is balanced? Study different menus from restaurants and think whether the options available are healthy or not. How could they be made healthier, e.g. grilled not fried, provide a sauce in a separate container

Main activity
Give the children time to design their menus and copy them up neat for display. Depending on the time of year you could suggest they have a theme for their menus such as, Christmas, spring, summer, Valentine's Day, etc.

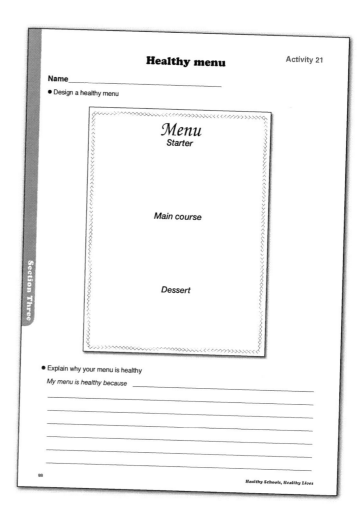

Plenary
The children should have an opportunity to show their menus to the class and explain why their menu is healthy. Ask the rest of the class do they agree?

Extension
Design a healthy birthday tea. How could you make it fun but still healthy? Ideas they could consider are vegetable sticks, low fat dips, sugar-free jelly, fresh fruit on cocktail sticks, smoothies, healthy sandwiches, rice cakes, plain pop-corn, etc.

Shopping list

Learning Objective
To consider healthy ingredients and long-term goals

Key Vocabulary
Ingredients, shopping, recipe,

Organisation
Whole class discussion and small group work of 4/5 children

Resources
● Recipe books

● 'Shopping list' activity sheet (one per child)

● 'Food pyramid activity sheet 1a (enlarge one copy)

● 'What do we eat?' activity sheet (one per group)

● Internet access

Introduction
Tell the children they will be working together in small groups to write a healthy shopping list. Explain they need to write down a list of food they would buy for a family of four (two adults and tow children).

Suggest they look through the recipe books to choose healthy low-fat meals. They need to decide what they are going to eat from Monday to Sunday, breakfast, lunch and dinner. They can write their ideas on the, 'What do we eat?' activity sheet.

Explain the occasional treat is allowed but to consider their choices sensibly. Emphasise they can not eat what they do not buy. Emphasis as well as learning how to eat healthily they should consider where to buy healthy food.

Main activity
Allow time for the children to look through the recipe books and consider healthy meals. They should discuss and produce a shopping list for their healthy meal or for a family of four for a week. Explain they need to ensure the cupboards are full of healthy foods such as oats, cans of tomatoes, fruit and vegetables, wholemeal rice and pasta.

Time could also be provided for groups of children to have access to the licence to cook website: www.licencetocook.org.uk/cooking.aspx. This website provides basic tutorials in cooking skills, eating, shopping and food hygiene with online assessments for each section to test the children's knowledge and understanding of these issues. The ideas compliment and support the skill of making a shopping list to feed a family of four.

Plenary
Ask for a spokesperson from each group to talk through their choices. The other groups can vote with a show of hands whether they think their shopping list is healthy or not.

Extension
Ask them to consider how their shopping list might differ if it were only for one person. How could they ensure a healthy diet if just cooking for themselves?

Good snacks bad snacks

Learning Objective

To identify food that is healthy and unhealthy

Key Vocabulary

Snacks, fast food, fresh food, options, choice

Organisation

Individual work at the child's own level

Resources

- 'Good snacks bad snacks' activity sheet (one per child)

- 'Instead of snacking' activity sheet (one per child)

Introduction

Explain to the class they are going to make lists of their favourite snacks that they eat on a regular basis. Tell the m they should be honest. Nobody needs to look at their list. The aim is for them to analyse their own eating habits as a starting point to help improve their own diets.

Main activity

Give out the 'Good snacks bad snacks' activity sheet. Explain after they have made their list they should sort the snacks they eat into two columns, 'good' and 'bad' snacks. Ask the children to think of alternatives to sweets and sugary snacks e.g. carrot and celery sticks, apples, bananas and salads.

Hand out the 'Instead of snacking' activity sheet and ask the children to think of ten things they could do instead of snacking when they are feeling bored or hungry. Explain these activities should be things that make it hard for them to eat whilst they are doing them, like roller skating or swimming.

Plenary

Ask the children to share their ideas with the rest of the class for both healthy snacks and their ideas for activities to do instead of snacking.

Extension

Make a healthy 'good snack, bad snack' display in the classroom to act as a reminder to the children when tempted to make bad choices.

Good snacks, bad snacks

Activity 23a

Name_____

- List your favourite snacks:

- Sort these snacks into the table below to show which ones are good healthy snacks and which ones are unhealthy snacks.

Good	Bad

- Are the snacks you eat mainly healthy or unhealthy? _____

- Write down some ideas for healthy alternatives to bad snacks.

Instead of snacking

Activity 23b

Name_____

- Write down ten things you could do instead of snacking when you're feeling bored or hungry.
- These activities should be things that make it hard for you to eat while you are doing them.

1. _____
2. _____
3. _____
4. _____
5. _____
6. _____
7. _____
8. _____
9. _____
10. _____

Healthy Schools, Healthy Lives

91

Section Three

Section Two

You are what you eat

Learning Objective
To understand that some food is good for us and some is not

Key Vocabulary
Arteries, blood pressure, cancer, stroke, illness, obesity, disease, cholesterol

Organisation
General class discussion and brainstorming and individual work at the child's own level

Resources
- 'You are what you eat – sheet one' activity sheet 24a (one per child)

- 'You are what you eat – sheet two' activity sheet 24b (one per child)

- Whiteboard or flipchart

- Marker pens

- Non-fiction books on obesity and related illnesses

Introduction
Explain that too much fat can kill us by clogging our arteries and weakening our hearts. Use the information in chapter two to discuss the long-term effects of eating the wrong foods and overeating. List some of these illnesses on a whiteboard or flip-chart so the children can refer to them during the lesson.

Main activity
Tell the children that a lot of fast food can be classed as fatty food and often is know as 'junk' food for this reason. Brainstorm other foods that could be classed a 'junk food' and list them on the whiteboard or a flip chart.

Hand out the 'You are what you eat – sheet one'. Explain they should put today's date above the image of the first body on this sheet. Encourage the class to draw sketches or labels of their favourite fatty foods around the first image of a body on the activity sheet. On the second image of the body they should draw or label the 'hidden' problems a fatty diet can cause. Suggest they date this one twenty years in the future.

Now give out the 'You are what you eat – sheet two'. Again they should put today's date above the image of the first body on this sheet. Encourage the class to draw sketches or labels of their favourite healthy foods around the first image of a body on this activity sheet. Suggest they date the second image of the body twenty years in the future. They should surround this image with sketches and labels of their favourite activities. Explain if they eat a healthy diet they will still be able to enjoy life doing these activities in twenty years time.

Plenary
Discuss the alternatives to junk food such as, boiling, grilling, baking, steaming, microwave. Reinforce the message that they should avoid fast foods and takeaways. Make a list of where they can buy healthy food.

Extension
The children can look up more information on obesity and illnesses related to obesity and make leaflets explaining the dangers of overeating.

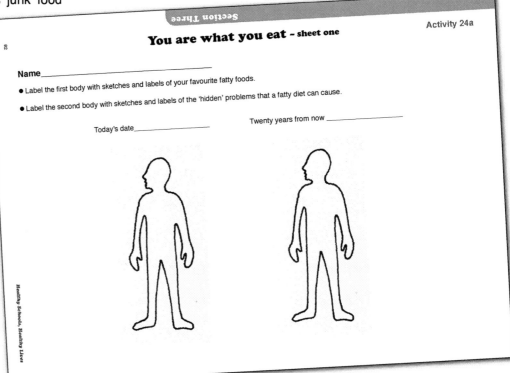

Section Three

You are what you eat – sheet one

Activity 24a

Name_____

- Label the first body with sketches and labels of your favourite fatty foods.

- Label the second body with sketches and labels of the 'hidden' problems that a fatty diet can cause.

Today's date_____   Twenty years from now _____

Healthy Schools, Healthy Lives

Section Two

A healthy debate

Learning Objective
To present a logical argument for or against fast food

Key Vocabulary
Fast food, junk food, healthy, unhealthy

Organisation
Small groups or 4 to five children

Resources
- 'A healthy debate' activity sheet (one per child)
- Internet access
- A1 paper
- Marker pens

Introduction
Explain to the class they are going to look at the pros and cons of eating fast food. Agree what is fast food. Does it include pre-prepared meals and tinned food from supermarkets or are you going to concentrate on takeaway food? Explain for this debate they are going to concentrate on takeaway food such as that bought in McDonalds, Burger King, KFC and Pizza Hut. Divide the class into small groups and then tell them whether they will be arguing in favour of fast food or against fast food.

Tell the children they have to support their opinions with facts. Allow time for them to look up some the fast food companies on the Internet and list some of the good things or bad things about the products they sell on the A1 paper. Point them in the direction of the main fast food company's websites who all provide information on the nutritional value of their food. The School food Trust website get real provides information on junk food including what they could be eating if they are not having a school lunch, www.getreal.uk.com.

Explain they are researching ideas to support their arguments. They can use pictures if they like.

Main activity
Each group should prevent their argument whilst the rest of the class watch as the audience. When they have finished they should vote on which group presented the best argument.

Ensure everyone involved listens carefully to all the arguments. Were their arguments based on experience, fact or opinion?

Plenary
Using the activity sheet 'A healthy debate', the children should write down some of the arguments they can remember to outline the pros and cons of fast food, using the two columns available.

Reinforce that the big fast food companies are all doing things to improve the health value of their food but, it is still not a good idea to have too many takeaways. It should be limited to special treats and not regular occurrences. It is important to emphasise that junk food may be a quick alternative, but it is not 'fun and trendy'. In excess it is very bad for their health and is often more expensive.

Extension
Examine the nutritional values of the four big fast food companies and compare the food values of different products to find out which is healthier. Here are web addresses for McDonald's, Burger King, Pizza Hut and KFC, which may be helpful but, you can choose any others you think are appropriate. www.mcdonalds.co.uk/food/nutrition/nutrition-counter.mcd, www.burgerking.co.uk/nutrition, www.kfc.co.uk/nutrition, www.pizzahut.co.uk/restaurants/menus--deals/dietary-information.aspx

---

A healthy debate

Activity 25

Name_____

- List the pros and cons of eating fast food

Pros	Cons

- Which argument do you agree with most? Why? _____

Section Three

94

Healthy Schools, Healthy Lives

Section Two

Learning Objective
To design a jingle or advert to persuade people to eat healthily

Key Vocabulary
Caption, catchphrase, jingle, persuasive, advertisement, healthy

Organisation
Small groups of three or four children

Resources
● A1 paper

● Food adverts recorded from TV and radio and found in magazines

● Recording of the NHS Change 4 life advert

● Jingles, activity sheet (one per child to record ideas and one for each group to use for brainstorming)

● Musical instruments

● Recording equipment

Introduction
Explain the media can effect what people choose to eat. Watch / listen to the adverts recorded from TV and the radio. Look at the food adverts in magazines to see what they are promoting. Are they promoting fast food? Sweets? Healthy salads? Is the food good or bad for their health? Tell the children there is often a marked discrepancy between the foods marketed at children and the nutritional quality of the food..

Tell the children that the Office of Communication (Ofcom) have introduced rules to ban advertising of junk food during TV programmes targeted at under-16s and on children,s channels. These rules came into effect in January 2007. This is because junk food is seen as part of the cause of our nation,s obesity problems.

Look at the NHS change 4 life advert. Ask the children what the Government is trying to promote Explain they are going to produce and record a jingle that would be suitable for a TV advert, or to be played on the radio that would persuade people to eat a healthy balanced diet or to exercise regularly. They can concentrate on one aspect of their diet, such as don,t eat fatty snacks between meals, drink plenty of water, eat their 5-a-day, check the fat, salt and sugar content in their food, etc.

Main activity
Look at the food adverts and discuss how different catchphrases are used. How do they relate to the product being advertised? Point out alliteration (beanz meanz Heinz) puns, rhythm (tell Œem about the honey

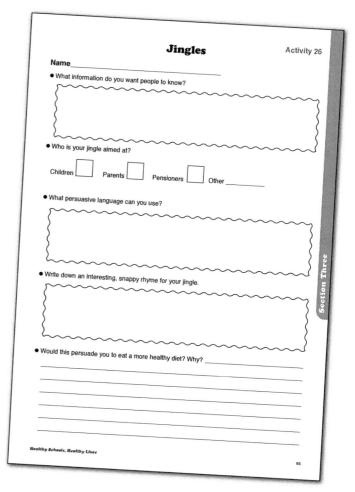

mummy) humour and word play. How would these work in a jingle or song? Look at the NHS advert and discuss how the Government is trying to put the message across by highlighting the negative effects of unhealthy living.

Produce jingles with percussion instruments that can be recorded, as if they were going to be used in a television advert or on the radio. The children could record their jingles and play them to the class or in an assembly.

Brainstorm own ideas for catchphrases on A1 paper in small groups. Think of an interesting snappy rhyme or poem for their jingle. Allow time for the groups to give each other constructive feedback about their jingles before they record them. Use percussion instruments to add a musical accompaniment to their jingle.

Plenary
Children should perform or play their jingles to the class. How do they grab your attention? Which ones stay in your memory? Why? What was special or unusual about the jingle, for example, jokes, music, caption?

Extension
Encourage the children to make posters to support their jingles to persuade people to eat a healthy diet a healthy lifestyle.

Moving about

Learning Objective
To recognise we can move in lots of different ways and moving helps burn off calories and reduce weight

Key Vocabulary
Hop, jump, crawl, run, walk, slide, skip, roll

Organisation
Whole class discussion, working with a partner and individual work

Resources
● 'Moving about' activity sheet (one per child)

● Hall

● PE kits

● PE Mats

Introduction
This activity sheet is designed to use with Year 3 or younger children. It will help them to realise how many ways they use their bodies to move and which parts of the body are involved. It is better to do the activity in a hall in PE kits than in the classroom or on the playground. If doing rolls it is an important health and safety feature to use the PE mats.

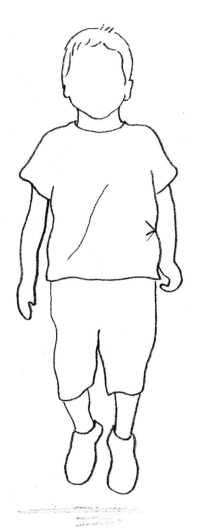

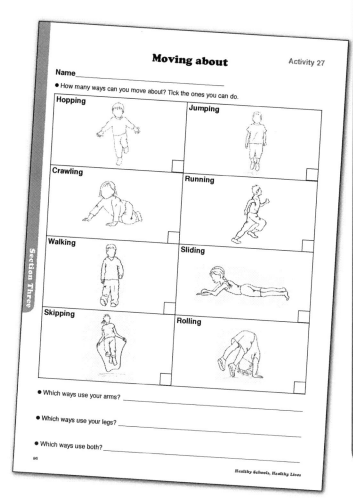

Explain to the class we are going to practice moving in different ways and think about what parts of our bodies we are moving.

Main activity
Ask the children to change into their PE kits and take them to the hall. Tell them they are going to move their bodies in different ways. Organise the class into pairs. Give out the activity sheets and pencils. Remind the children to put the pencils down before they start exercising.

Call out the different ways of moving shown on the activity sheet and their partner checks if they can do it. If their partner is happy they can move in the specified way they can tick the box.

Ask them to work out with their partner which ways use their arms, which ways use their legs and which ways use both. Write down their findings on the sheet.

Plenary
Back in the classroom, share what they found out about the way they move. Explain running, jumping, skipping and walking are all ways they can exercise their bodies.

Extension
How many different types of jumps can you do? What other ways can you think of to move on different parts of your body? Why is it important to exercise?

Section Two

Section Three

Physical activity and our heart

Learning Objective
To learn that an increased heart rate helps the oxygen move around our bodies

Key Vocabulary
Pulse rate, heart rate, resting, active,

Organisation
Working in small groups of about four children

Resources
- 'Physical activity and our heart' activity sheet (one per group)

- PE Kits

- Hall time

- 10-minute timer

- Copy of chart

Introduction
Explain the heart is a muscle that pumps the blood around the body. The muscles in the body need blood, which carries oxygen. Muscles need oxygen to work. Tell the children how to take their pulse rate by placing their finger next to the tendon on wrist. Practise taking pulse rates by counting the beats for 30 seconds and doubling it to give a pulse rate in beats per minute (bpm).

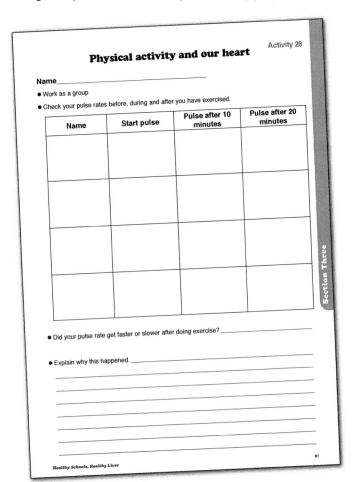

Before you start the PE lesson ask the children to take their resting pulse. Ensure they write their resting pulse rate down. Children should undertake normal PE activities, not attempt to 'test' their stamina or strength. Ensure the children who need inhalers have them readily available.

Main activity
Carry out a normal PE lesson and encourage the children to work quite hard. After about 10 minutes ask the children to take their pulse again and write it down. Allow time to complete the activity sheet.

Continue the lesson and after about 20 minutes of vigorous exercise during a normal PE lesson, ask the children to take their pulse rate again. If desired you could also ask the children to take their pulse after the warm-down to compare the difference.

Plenary
Did their pulse rate get faster or slower after doing exercise?

Tell the children blood carries oxygen around the body. We can tell how fast our heart is beating from our pulse. Our pulse increases when we exercise because our muscles need more oxygen.
Explain this is because the heart beats faster with exercise to get more oxygen to muscles in motion. Our hearts beat slower when we are resting because our muscles are less active.

Extension
Did our heart rate get faster or slower when we exercised? Why? Would the results have been the same if a very fit athlete had carried out the same experiment? Why?

Healthy Schools, Healthy Lives

Section Two

Check your pulse

Learning Objective
To recognise that we need exercise to stay healthy

Key Vocabulary
Pulse, heart, bpm, exercise, weight, investigate

Organisation
Whole class activity and individual work at the child's own level

Resources
- 'Check your pulse' activity sheet (one per child)
- PE kits
- Hall time
- Stop watches
- Selection of sports equipment available such as, skipping ropes, quoits, bean bags, small and large balls, cones, etc.

Introduction
Remind the children how to find their pulse in their wrist. In pairs, ask them to time each other for a minute taking their pulse. How many beats can they count in a minute?

Explain they are going to plan and carry out their own science investigation to find out what sort of exercise effects pulse rate. Ask them what forms of exercise they can think of. How do they think these exercises would affect their pulse rate? How could they measure it? How could they record their results?

Explain to the children they should undertake normal types of PE activities and not attempt to 'test' their stamina and strength. Ensure they have their inhalers readily available if they should need them.

Main activity
Now ask them to time for fifteen seconds and multiply by four to get their average pulse rate.

Explain this will also show them how many beats to the minute.

Ask the children to find out if their pulse rate stays higher longer if they exercise longer. What variables would need to stay the same? What variables would need to change? How could they make it a fair test?

Remind the children that regular exercise can help burn calories and reduce weight. Any increase in activity will help, such as walking, cycling and using the stairs instead of going in the lift. Physical activity is essential for good health at all ages.

Plenary
Back in the classroom, discuss the questions on the 'Check your pulse' activity sheet. Allow time for the children to complete the activity sheet after the discussion.

Explain our pulse rate increases whilst we are exercising because our muscles need more oxygen, when we stop exercising our pulse rates return to normal.

Extension
Are everybody's pulse rates the same? Are their pulse rates the same as each other?
What sort of exercise effects pulse rate?

To increase awareness of the amount of activity they do in a day you could issue pedometers to the class to see how many steps they do during the school day. If there are not enough pedometers in school for one each, choose a few volunteers who can report back to the class at the end of the day. Walking 10,000 steps a day can build stamina, burn excess calories and give you a healthier heart.

Pulse rate activity sheet

Pulse rate — Activity 29

Name_____

- What exercises do you enjoy? _____

- What did you feel like after exercising, e.g. tired, out of breath, hot?
  After exercising I feel ... _____

- How does this compare to when you are sitting still?
  When I sit still I feel ... _____

- What happened to your pulse rate after exercising?
  After exercising my pulse rate ... _____

- Was this what you thought would happen?
  I thought ... _____

- Does your pulse rate stay higher for longer if you exercise longer?
  If I exercise for longer my pulse rate ... _____

Healthy Schools, Healthy Lives

98

Section Two

Section Three

How do our muscles work?

Learning Objective
To understand exercise increases stamina, maintains muscles and improves general health

Key Vocabulary
Muscles, healthy, health, exercise, resting, relaxing, working

Organisation
Whole class demonstration and individual work at the child's own level.

Resources
● 'Muscles' activity sheet (one per child)

● 'Bones' activity sheet (one per child)

● 5-minute timer

● Balls

● Skipping ropes

● Beanbags

Introduction
Muscles are used whenever you move. Without muscles we would not be able to walk, run or even eat our food. There are over 650 muscles in the body, which makes up half a persons body weight.

Ask the children if they think their muscles work harder during exercise or when they are sitting still? What muscles do they use when they are running? Walking? Standing? Brushing their teeth? Muscles are made of threads and connected to the bones with tendons. The adult human body has 206 bones.

Main activity
Ask the children to sit at their table with their elbow on the table and lean their head on their fist. Gently squeeze the front of their upper arm, half way between the shoulder and the elbow. Tell them this is a muscle under their skin and it is called a bicep. What does their bicep feel like - soft and relaxed, or hard and firm? Explain the muscle is at rest and not working.

Now ask them to sit at their table and, in turn, they should put one hand under the edge of the table and carefully try to lift it a few centimetres from the floor. With their other hand ask the children to feel their bicep. What has happened to it now? Are their biceps soft and relaxed, or hard and firm?

Next feel the muscle in the lower half of the leg. This is called the calf. Ask the children to jog on the spot for five minutes using the timer. What do their calves feel like now?

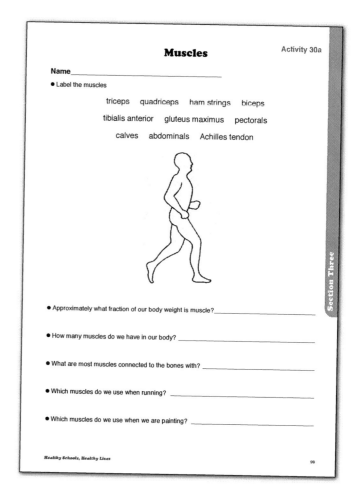

Ask the children to label the muscles and bones using the 'Muscles' and 'Bones' activity sheets.

Plenary
What does this tell you about your muscles? Explain muscles help your bones moves.

Reinforce that when a muscle is working it is firm and when it is relaxed it is soft. Tell the children that when someone is exercising or moving fast, the muscles work hard. Explain the muscle feels hotter because it has been working hard. It is important to stretch muscles before exercise to warm them up.

A proper warm-up can increase the blood flow to the working muscle which results in decreased muscle stiffness, less risk of injury and improved performance. Doing the right exercises can help burn off fat and build muscle.

Extension
The children could devise their own experiment for testing the muscles.

Town planning

Learning Objective
To demonstrate an understanding of the needs of the community when staying fit and healthy

Key Vocabulary
Community, structured and unstructured play, cycle paths, park, recreation

Organisation
Group discussion and individual work

Resources
● 'Town planning' activity sheet (one per child)

● 'Adventure playground' activity sheet (one per child)

Introduction
Tell the children they are going to design their own town. The philosophy of the town is to be active and keep fit. What sporting facilities could they include in their town? Suggest ideas like bowling, ice-skating, swimming, football, cricket, adventure playgrounds, dance halls, etc.

The idea is to encourage travel such as cycling, walking, the use of parks and green spaces and promoting opportunities for active unstructured play. Tell the children they should include a safe route to school which would be suitable for walking and cycling. Explain to the class that providing adequate bicycle sheds to store the children's bicycles and scooters will encourage the children to ride their bikes to school.

Encourage them to include cycle paths and recreational facilities where the children can run, climb, swim and get exercise in structured and unstructured environments. Explain that structured and unstructured play is vitally important to children's physical and emotional well being.

Main activity
Draw a town showing plenty of facilities suitable to encourage more physical activity for all ages.

Plenary
Ask for volunteers to tell the rest or the class about their town designs. How does it promote a healthy lifestyle?

Extension
Design an adventure playground. If you want you could specify an age limit for this activity or let the children have free-range for their imaginations to run-wild. They could make it a themed adventure playground if they wish, such as pirates, space or the jungle.

Section Two

Town planning　　　　　　　　　　　Activity 31a

Healthy Schools, Healthy Lives

Name_____

● Design your own town. Think how you could encourage people to get more exercise.

● How does your town encourage a healthy lifestyle? _____

_____

_____

_____

101

Section Three

Being healthy

Learning Objective
To demonstrate an understanding of why it is good to be healthy

Key Vocabulary
Physical activity, sports, adventure playground, dancing, swimming,

Organisation
Whole class discussion, group work and individual consolidation

Resources
- 'Being healthy' activity sheet (one per child)

- A1 paper

- Marker pens

Introduction
Brainstorm ways with the children they can increase their physical activity and reduce their physical inactivity. Make lists which can be displayed around the classroom. Here are some to get you started:

Tips to increase physical activity:
- Encourage walking to places such as school and the shops, rather than always jumping in the car or bus. Doctors recommend a gradual increase in physical activity, such as brisk walking, to at least an hour a day.

- Suggest going to the park for a kick around with a football, or a game of rounders, cricket or Frisbee.

- Visit a local leisure centre to investigate sports and team activities to get involved in.

- Make exercise into a treat by taking special trips to an adventure play park or an ice skating rink, for example. Involve the whole family in bike rides, swimming and in-line skating. www.bupa.co.uk

Build activity into your daily life:
- Young at heart - Physical activity helps keep your heart strong and healthy

- Stressed? Aaargh!! - Physical activity lifts your mood, reduces stress levels and helps you sleep

- Keep it simple - Walking is a great way to build activity into your daily routine; use a pedometer and take 10,000 steps a day

- Going Up? - Instead of taking the lift or the escalators use the stairs

- Get the right kit, but don't spend a fortune - Get yourself some comfy trainers, a pair of tracksuit bottoms, and a t-shirt

- Join a club - this will help with regular activity and it's also a great place to meet new friends

- Why not try something new? - Have you ever thought of rollerblading, salsa dancing or martial arts.

- It fit's!! - Make activity a regular part of your routine. Why not join a lunchtime exercise class or go for a swim before school.

- It takes two - Having an activity buddy will keep you motivated and make it more enjoyable

- Try dancing - Its fun, you can do it anywhere and it burns up lots of calories. www.gethealthycov.org.uk/

Reducing physical inactivity:
- Average time spent in front of the TV or PC and what they could do instead

- Importance of sleep - Sleep diary

Activity sheet

Being healthy Activity 32

Name_____

- List the reasons why it is good to be healthy and bad to be unhealthy

Good things about Healthy	Bad things about being Unhealthy

- List three ways you can change the way you eat to improve your health:

- List three ways you can increase the amount of physical activity you do to improve your health:

Healthy Schools, Healthy Lives

103

- Tips to reduce physical inactivity:

- Physically inactive pastimes such as watching TV or playing computer games should be limited to around two hours a day or an average of 14 hours a week.

- Encourage children to be selective about what they watch and concentrate only on the programmes they really enjoy. www.bupa.co.uk

Main activity

Talk about why it is good to be healthy. Emphasise it is no good saying you will do it later, or start next month. We need to change our lifestyles now to make a difference. Here are some ideas to help the discussion:

Good things about being Healthy	Bad things about being Unhealthy
Become better able to play sports Become a faster runner Feel better about myself Like the way I look in clothes Be better able to find clothes I like Find that other people will like me more Undergo less teasing from others Feel proud of myself Feel stronger See parents become proud Spend less money on food Save money for other things Understand myself better	Takes a lot of time to lose weight Might feel worse if I fail Others might laugh at me for dieting Others might get mad at me for not eating like they do Might change my view of myself Will be hard to keep myself from eating foods I like

Ask the children to make their own list of good things about being healthy and bad things about being unhealthy in small groups on the A1 paper.

Plenary

Ask for a spokesperson from each group to share and their ideas. Encourage the children to record some of these ideas on the 'Being healthy' activity sheet.

Extension

Some of the children might like to write their own eating and keeping fit board game on large sheets of paper that covers everything they have learnt. These board games could be given to the other children to play.

Extra-curricular activities

Cycle Proficiency

The government aims to increase cycling across the nation by 8% in 2012.

UK's National Cyclists' Organisation (CTC) and The Royal Society for the Prevention of Accidents (RoSPA) have joined together with the Department for Transport to create a new National Standard for Cycle Training. This involves training for children and adults, in real situations under the supervision of qualified instructors.

The majority of schools in the UK undertake the National Cycle Proficiency Test (NCPS). It is believed that by teaching basic road sense at an early age will lay a good foundation for their future as safe road users - after all - today's child cyclist is tomorrow's young driver. It is ideal for encouraging a future skill that will keep people fit from an early age and will help to tackle the obesity problem.

The test includes on-road training, usually over a six week period. During that time children learn:

- The importance of cycle maintenance

- The Highway Code for the Young Road User

- Manoeuvring safely through obstacles

- Riding safely on the road

Gardening club

Gardening clubs are becoming very popular in school and can include vegetable growing, an allotment for each class, growing fruit and vegetables in a green house and an orchard. They are ideal for teaching children how to grow their own produce, as well as being an ideal form of exercise.

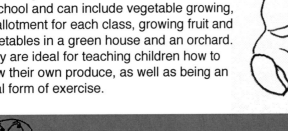

Cooking club

In January 2008, as part of the Government's obesity strategy, Secretary of State for Children, Schools and Families, Ed Balls, announced that cookery lessons would be made compulsory in secondary schools for 11- to 14-year-olds.

"Leaving school able to cook healthy dishes from scratch is an essential everyday skill all young people should have," he said. "It is at the heart of tackling obesity."

Understanding the importance of healthy eating, "is meaningless without the skills to put these messages into practice."

Primary schools can help to focus children's interest in healthy eating, nutrition and food hygiene by setting up cookery clubs. This is a great way to teach children the fundamentals of healthy meals and healthy eating. The skills children learn will be beneficial for the rest of their life. Some schools may already be involved in the Lets Get Cooking Scheme, see chapter one for more details.

Sports clubs

It is the responsibility of the school to ensure that there is a wide range of sports clubs available for children to participate in. The more choices there are available, the more opportunities for exercise and for working together to combat obesity. This can include: football, cricket, rugby, netball and athletics, etc.

A good idea is to ask the children at school what other sports clubs they partake in. The addresses and details of these clubs could be shared with parents in newsletters and will encourage all children to get more exercise. Education departments of local authorities are responsible for many locally available sports facilities. You can contact them or visit their websites for more information.

Photocopiable Sheets

This Section contains the photocopiable activity sheets outlined in Section Two. There are 32 activities with 39 photocopiable worksheets, which can be used in the classroom or set as homework.

Section Three

Food pyramid

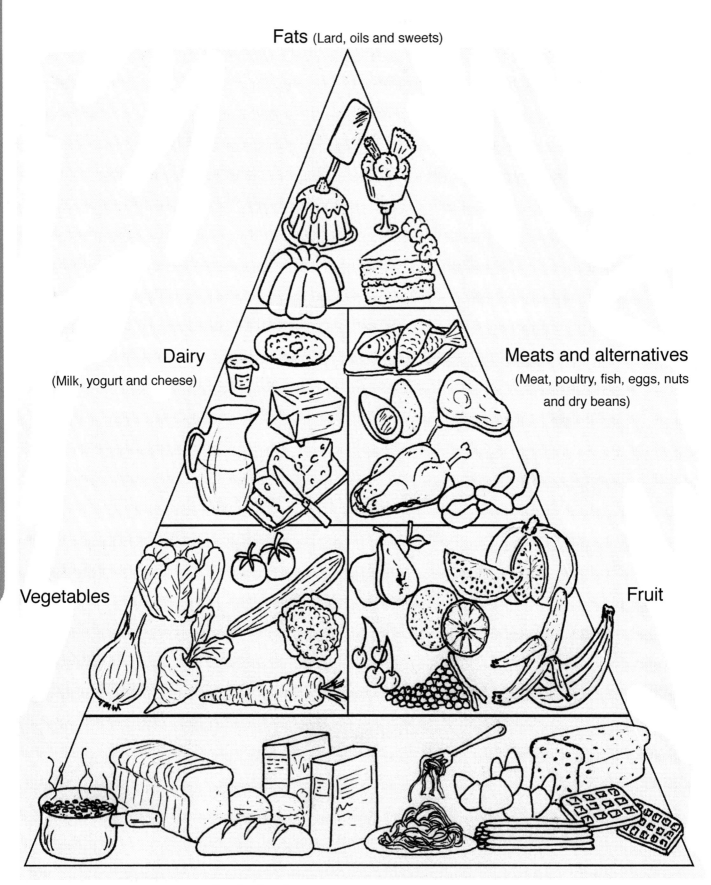

Fats (Lard, oils and sweets)

Dairy
(Milk, yogurt and cheese)

Meats and alternatives
(Meat, poultry, fish, eggs, nuts
and dry beans)

Vegetables

Fruit

Carbohydrates (Bread, cereals, rice and pasta)

Section Three

Photocopiable

Healthy Schools, Healthy Lives

Food pyramid

Name_____

● Complete the food pyramid by drawing or cutting out pictures and sticking on the different food types in the right places and label them

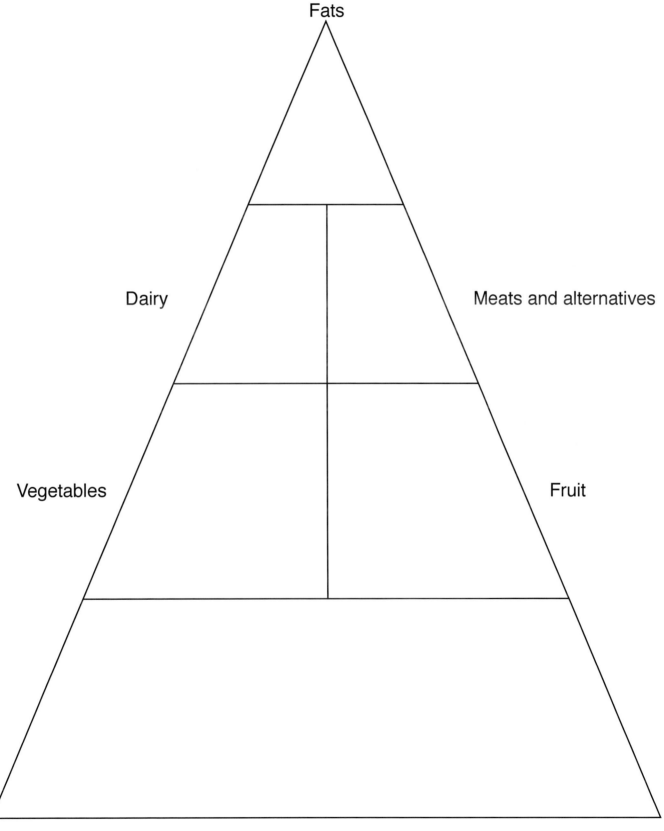

Fats

Dairy

Meats and alternatives

Vegetables

Fruit

Carbohydrates

Section Three

What do we eat?

Name_____

● Put a tick by the foods you think are healthy and a cross by the ones you think are not healthy

Pie with chips

Spaghetti bolognaise

Fried breakfast

Fish, new potatoes and vegetables

Teacle sponge pudding

Fruit salad

Fruit jelly

Slice of chocolate cake

Section Three

What do we eat?

Name _____

Day	Monday	Tuesday	Wednesday	Thursday	Friday	Saturday	Sunday
Breakfast							
Lunch							
Dinner							
Snacks							
Exercise							

Section Three

Breakfast survey

Name_____

● Keep a record of what you eat for breakfast over the week.

Monday _____

Tuesday _____

Wednesday _____

Thursday _____

Friday _____

Saturday _____

Sunday _____

● Draw a bar to show the different kinds of breakfasts you ate.

Amount eaten								
1								
2								
3								
4								
5								
6								
7								
	NONE							

Type of breakfast eaten

● Which is the most popular breakfast? _____

● Was it a healthy option? Why?_____

_____

_____

_____

● Why is it important to eat breakfast? _____

_____

_____

Photocopiable *Healthy Schools, Healthy Lives*

Section Three

Meals in a day

Name_____

● Draw what you would eat in a typical day.

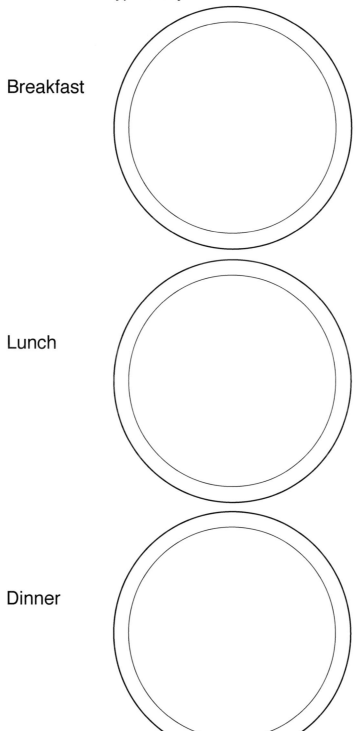

Breakfast

Lunch

Dinner

● Which meal is the healthiest? Why? _____

_____

_____

_____

Healthy eating

Name_____

● Look at the list of foods below:

banana   kidney beans   ice cream

sweets   leeks   chips   crisps   salmon

chocolate   cheese   fish fingers   sausages

sticky toffee pudding   yogurt   chicken and mushroom pie

milk   burgers   plums   pizza

tin tomatoes   jelly   new potatoes   dumplings

lamb chops   carrots

● Which are healthy and which are not healthy? Put them in the correct column on the table.

Healthy	Not healthy
Why are these healthy foods? _____ _____ _____ _____	**Why are these unhealthy foods?** _____ _____ _____ _____

Section Three

A healthy balanced meal

Name _____

- Draw a healthy balanced meal on the plate and explain why it is healthy.

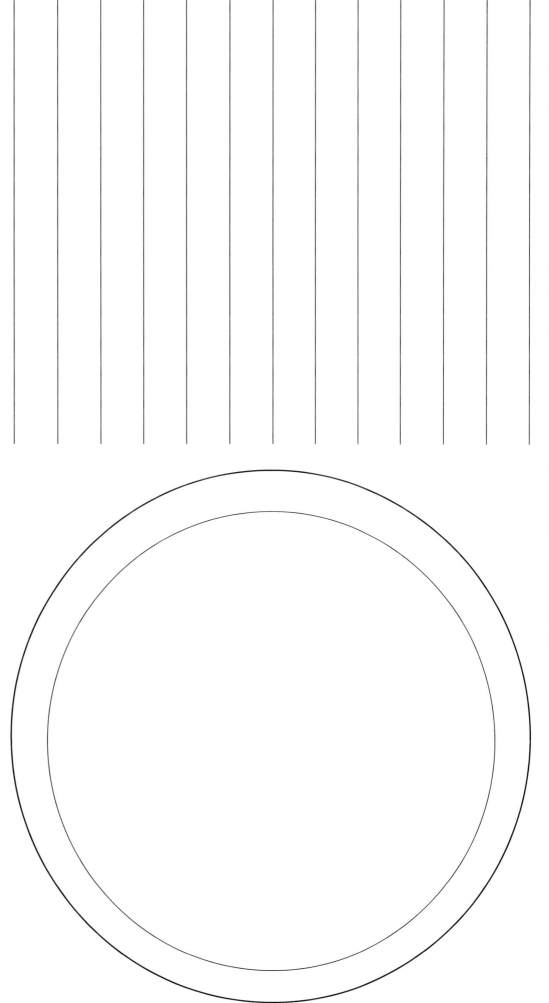

A healthy balanced meal

Name

● Draw a healthy balanced meal on the plate and explain why it is healthy.

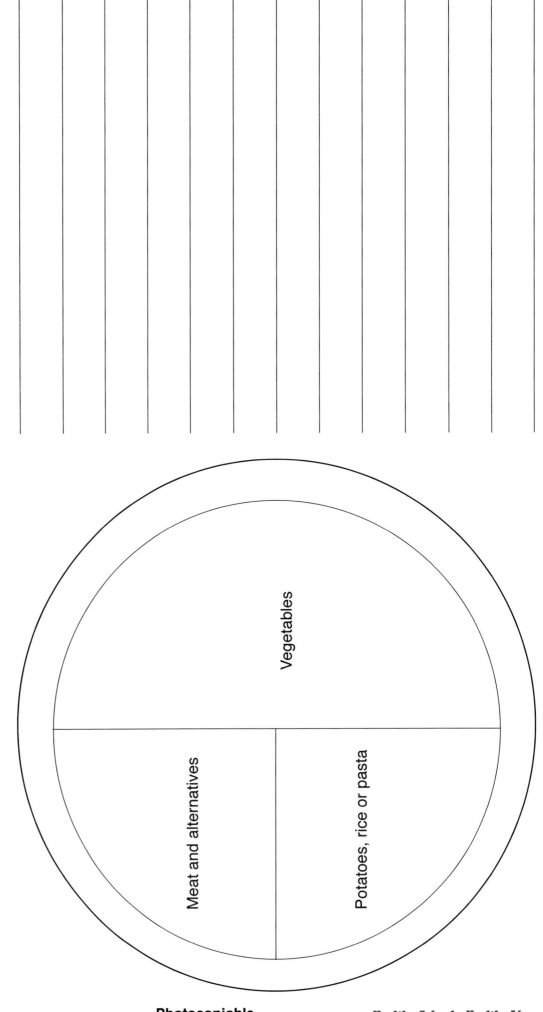

Vegetables

Meat and alternatives

Potatoes, rice or pasta

Photocopiable

Healthy Schools, Healthy Lives

A rainbow of food

Name _____

● Draw and write as many different fruit and vegetables as you can to make a rainbow of food.

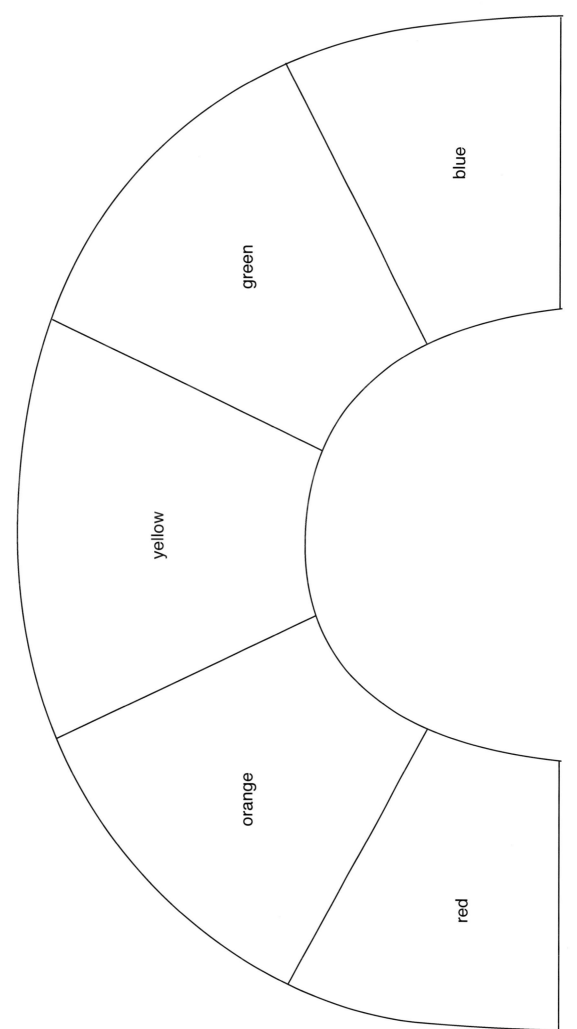

Fruit and veg around the world

Name

● Label the map to show where your favourite fruit and vegetables come from.

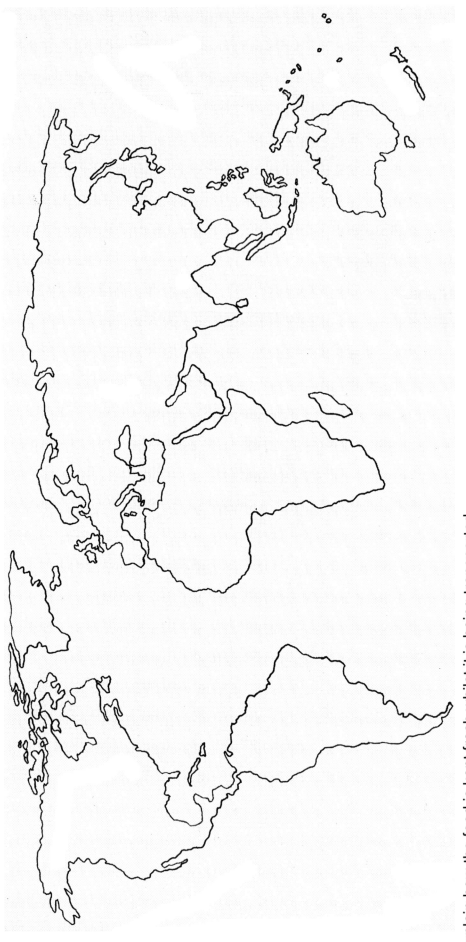

● Explain how the food is kept fresh whilst it is being transported.

Photocopiable

Healthy Schools, Healthy Lives

Fruit and vegetable tasting

Name_____

- Taste a selection of different fruit and vegetables

- Complete the chart

Like	Dislike

- Add any other fruit and vegetables you know you like to the chart.

- What are your top five favourite fruits: _____

_____

_____

_____

- What are your top five favourite vegetables: _____

_____

_____

_____

Section Three

Eat your 5 a day

Name_____

● Design and make a poster to persuade people to eat five different fruits and vegetables a day

Photocopiable   *Healthy Schools, Healthy Lives*

Design a smoothie

Name_____

● Design a healthy fruit smoothie.

Name your smoothie

_____

Ingredients: _____

_____

_____

_____

_____

_____

_____

How to make the smoothie:_____

_____

_____

_____

● What did you like most about your smoothie? _____

_____

_____

● What would you change?_____

_____

Drink 8 a day

Name_____

● Design a poster to remind people to drink enough water every day

● How much water have you drunk so far today?

Photocopiable

Healthy Schools, Healthy Lives

Section Three

Healthy sandwich

Name_____

● Design a healthy balanced sandwich.

Carbohydrates	Dairy	Protein	Fruit and Veg	Fats and sugars

● Name your sandwich _____

● How did you make your sandwich? _____

_____

_____

_____

_____

● What did you like most about your sandwich?_____

_____

_____

_____

● What would you change?_____

_____

_____

_____

Healthy lunchbox

Name_____

● What would you include in a healthy lunchbox?

● Draw and label the food items in your healthy lunchbox.

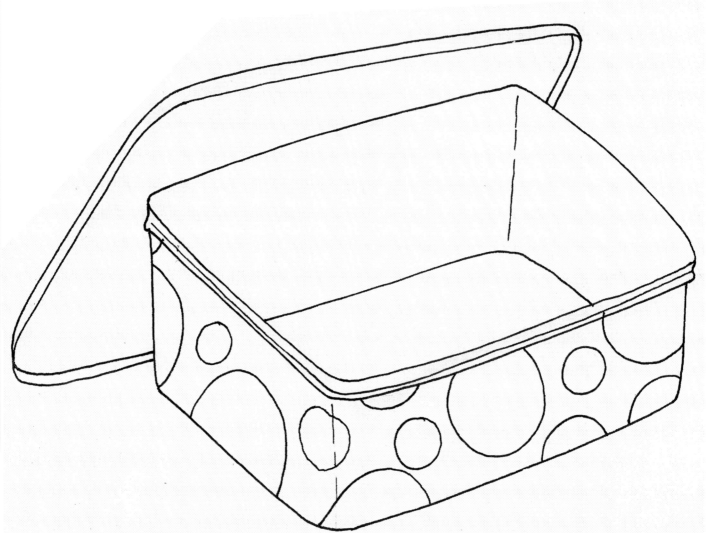

● Explain why the items in your lunchbox are healthy? _____

_____

_____

_____

Photocopiable   *Healthy Schools, Healthy Lives*

Portion size

Name_____

Food type	Portion of ...		Size	
Carbohydrates (6-11 servings a day)		Cereal	fist	
		Pancake	CD	
		Pasta/rice/potato	tennis ball	
		Bread	cassette tape case	
Fruit and vegetables (5 a day)		Salad	tennis ball	
		Fruit	tennis ball	
		Vegetables	tennis ball	
		Raisins	Large egg	
Dairy (2-3 servings a day)		Cheese	small matchbox	
		Ice-cream	tennis ball	
		Milk	fist	
		Yogurt	fist	
Meat and alternatives (2-4 servings a day)		Meat/poultry	deck of cards	
		Grilled fish	chequebook	
		Dried beans	large egg	
Fats (Use sparingly)		Oil	teaspoon	
		Jam	teaspoon	

Section Three

Portion distortion

Name_____

- Compare the portion sizes between food twenty-five years ago and today.

- Estimate the calories in the food today

- Tick how much exercise is needed to burn off these calories

25 years ago	Today	Exercise needed to burn off calories
Small burger 300 calories	Large Burger _____calories	30 minutes 1 hour 1 hour 30 minutes 2 hours
Old fashioned bottle of fizzy drink 85 calories	Two litre plastic bottle of fizzy drink _____calories	30 minutes 1 hour 1 hour 30 minutes 2 hours
Small muffin 200 calories	Large muffin _____calories	30 minutes 1 hour 1 hour 30 minutes 2 hours
Box of popcorn 250 calories	Tub of popcorn _____calories	30 minutes 1 hour 1 hour 30 minutes 2 hours

Section Three

Plaque attack

Name_____

● What were we testing?_____

_____

● What did we do? _____

_____

_____

_____

_____

● What did you observe?

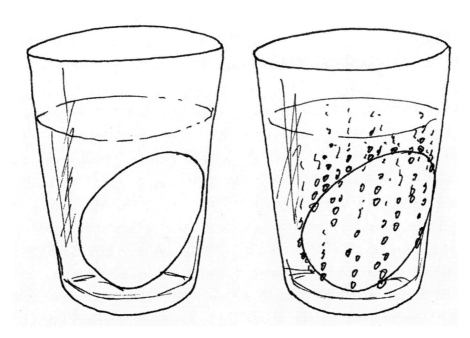

● What does this mean for your teeth? _____

_____

_____

_____

_____

_____

Section Three

Dental health

Name_____

● Work with a partner to count the number of teeth you have.

● Mark the missing teeth with a cross (x) and any fillings with an 'F'.

Maxillary Teeth

1 Central incisor

2 Lateral incisor

3 Canine

4 First premolar

5 Second premolar

6 First molar

7 Second molar

8 Third molar

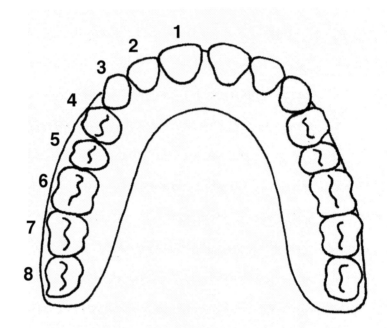

Mandibular Teeth

9 Third molar

10 Second molar

11 First molar

12 Second premolar

13 First premolar

14 Canine

15 Lateral incisor

16 Central incisor

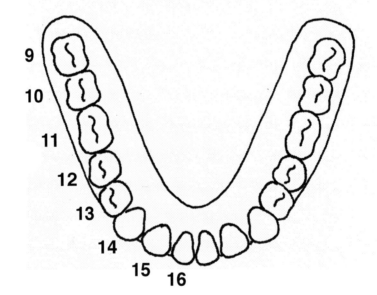

● What did you find out about your teeth after taking the disclosure tablet?_____

_____

_____

_____

_____

_____

Photocopiable *Healthy Schools, Healthy Lives*

Nutritional facts

Name _____

- Look at the nutritional values on the wrappers of different foods. Complete the table.

Items	Calories	Sugar	Fats	Saturates	Salt	Healthy	Reason why?

- Tick the items you think are healthy

- Write the reasons you think these items are healthy or why you think they are not healthy.

Section Three

Traffic lights

Name_____

● Classify the different foods according to the traffic light system.

● Give reasons for your choices

Red

I think these foods are red because…

_____
_____
_____
_____
_____
_____
_____

Amber

I think these foods are amber because…

_____
_____
_____
_____
_____
_____

Green

I think these foods are green because…

_____
_____
_____
_____
_____
_____

Photocopiable   *Healthy Schools, Healthy Lives*

Healthy menu

Name_____

● Design a healthy menu

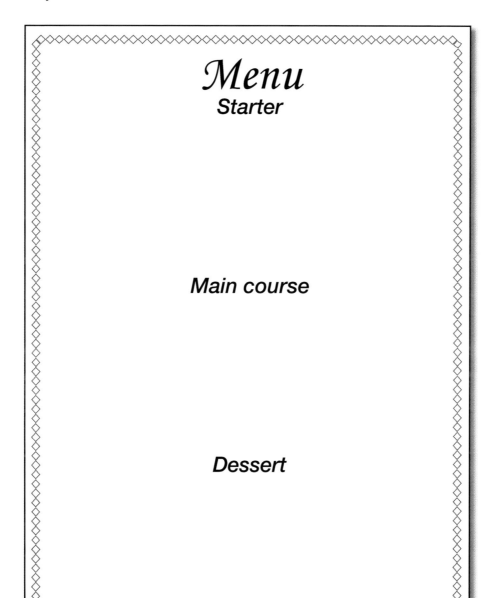

Menu
Starter

Main course

Dessert

● Explain why your menu is healthy

My menu is healthy because _____

_____

_____

_____

_____

_____

Shopping list

Name_____

● Write a shopping list of healthy foods to feed your family for a week

Shopping List

Photocopiable

Healthy Schools, Healthy Lives

Good snacks, bad snacks

Name_____

● List your favourite snacks:

_____

_____

_____

_____

_____

_____

● Sort these snacks into the table below to show which ones are good healthy snacks and which ones are unhealthy snacks.

Good	Bad

● Are the snacks you eat mainly healthy or unhealthy? _____

● Write down some ideas for healthy alternatives to bad snacks.

_____

_____

_____

_____

_____

_____

_____

Section Three

Instead of snacking

Name_____

● Write down ten things you could do instead of snacking when you're feeling bored or hungry.

● These activities should be things that make it hard for you to eat while you are doing them.

1. _____

2. _____

3. _____

4. _____

5. _____

6. _____

7. _____

8. _____

9. _____

10. _____

Photocopiable

Healthy Schools, Healthy Lives

You are what you eat – sheet one

Section Three

Name _____

● Label the first body with sketches and labels of your favourite fatty foods.

● Label the second body with sketches and labels of the 'hidden' problems that a fatty diet can cause.

Today's date _____

Twenty years from now _____

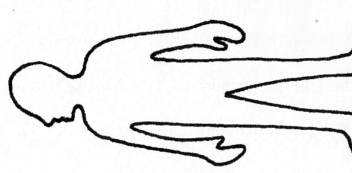

You are what you eat sheet two

Name _____

● Label the first body with sketches and labels of your favourite healthy foods.

● Label the second body with sketches and labels of activities you will still be able to enjoy in twenty years time.

Today's date _____

Twenty years from now _____

Photocopiable

Healthy Schools, Healthy Lives

A healthy debate

Name

● List the pros and cons of eating fast food

Pros	Cons

● Which argument do you agree with most? Why?

Photocopiable

Section Three

Jingles

Name_____

- What information do you want people to know?

- Who is your jingle aimed at?

Children ☐   Parents ☐   Pensioners ☐   Other _____

- What persuasive language can you use?

- Write down an interesting, snappy rhyme for your jingle.

- Would this persuade you to eat a more healthy diet? Why? _____

_____

_____

_____

_____

_____

    Photocopiable   *Healthy Schools, Healthy Lives*

Section Three

Moving about

Name_____

● How many ways can you move about? Tick the ones you can do.

Hopping	Jumping
Crawling	Running
Walking	Sliding
Skipping	Rolling

● Which ways use your arms? _____

● Which ways use your legs? _____

● Which ways use both? _____

Physical activity and our heart

Name_____

- Work as a group

- Check your pulse rates before, during and after you have exercised.

Name	Start pulse	Pulse after 10 minutes	Pulse after 20 minutes

- Did your pulse rate get faster or slower after doing exercise?_____

- Explain why this happened. _____

_____

_____

_____

_____

_____

_____

Photocopiable

Healthy Schools, Healthy Lives

Section Three

Pulse rate

Name_____

- What exercises do you enjoy? _____

_____

_____

- What did you feel like after exercising, e.g. tired, out of breath, hot?

After exercising I feel … _____

_____

_____

- How does this compare to when you are sitting still?

When I sit still I feel … _____

_____

_____

- What happened to your pulse rate after exercising?

After exercising my pulse rate … _____

_____

_____

- Was this what you thought would happen?

I thought … _____

_____

_____

- Does your pulse rate stay higher for longer if you exercise longer?

If I exercise for longer my pulse rate … _____

_____

_____

Section Three

Muscles

Name_____

● Label the muscles

triceps   quadriceps   ham strings   biceps

tibialis anterior   gluteus maximus   pectorals

calves   abdominals   Achilles tendon

● Approximately what fraction of our body weight is muscle?_____

● How many muscles do we have in our body? _____

● What are most muscles connected to the bones with? _____

● Which muscles do we use when running? _____

● Which muscles do we use when we are painting? _____

Bones

Name_____

● Label the skeleton

rib   femur   radius   tibia   pelvis

skull   ulna   humerus   fibula

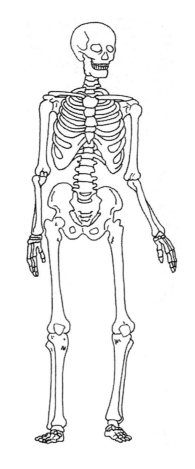

● Which bones do we move when jumping?_____

● Which bones do we move when running? _____

● Which bones do we move when painting? _____

● Which bones protect our heart?_____

● How many bones are there in the human body? _____

Town planning

Name

● Design your own town. Think how you could encourage people to get more exercise.

● How does your town encourage a healthy lifestyle?

Photocopiable

Healthy Schools, Healthy Lives

Adventure playground

Name

● Design your own adventure playground.

● Explain the main features of your playground

Section Three

Being healthy

Name_____

● List the reasons why it is good to be healthy and bad to be unhealthy

Good things about Healthy	Bad things about being Unhealthy

● List three ways you can change the way you eat to improve your health:

_____

_____

_____

● List three ways you can increase the amount of physical activity you do to improve your health:

_____

_____

_____

Photocopiable *Healthy Schools, Healthy Lives*

Individual health plan

Name _____ DOB _____ Class _____ Stage _____

Strengths (curricular, extra-curricular and preferred learning styles)

Areas to be developed (targets should address these needs)

Pastoral and Medical Arrangements

Targets	Strategies and Resources	Provision - Who and When?	Success Criteria/ Evaluation

Monitoring and assessment arrangements

Pupil's contribution and views

Parent/carer involvement and comments

Strategies and activities for home, home/school link arrangements

Signed: **Review Date :**

Summary evaluation and future action – successful strategies, progress, concerns, issues, next steps etc.

Section Three

My individual health plan

Name _____ DOB _____ Class _____ Stage _____

I am good at:

Start Date: | **Review Date:**

Learning Targets	How will I know when I have reached my target?	How am I doing?			

What did I do well?

What do I need to do next?

Photocopiable

Healthy Schools, Healthy Lives

Useful contacts log

	Named person	Phone number	Email
Teacher			
SEN coordinator			
Local/regional obesity lead			
Regional healthy schools coordinator			
School nurse			
Health centre/doctor			
Mend			

Glossary

Balanced diet
Foods eaten that provide all the essential nutrients in the appropriate amounts to support life processes, such as growth in children without promoting excess weight gain

BMI
Body Mass Index is a person's weight (kg) divided by the square of their height (m). It is used by medical practitioners to determine if a person's weight is within a healthy range

Carbohydrates
Starchy foods that can be converted readily into glucose to provide energy to the body

Bullying
Deliberate, hurtful behaviour repeated over a period of time

Calorie
Unit of food energy obtained from food and drink

Cholesterol
Fatty substance found in the body an excess of which can cause heart disease

Chronic
Lasting a long time

Dehydration
A lack of water in the body which causes a feeling of weakness

Depression
Illness that involves the body, mood, and thoughts, that affects the way a person eats and sleeps, the way one feels about oneself, and the way one thinks about things

Diet
The food a person regularly eats

Dietary reference values (DRV's)
Recommended nutrient values for different groups of individuals

Dietician
Someone who advices people about what they eat

Energy
Essential fuel for all body processes

Epidemic
Condition that is occurring more frequently and extensively among individuals in a community or population than is expected.

Food allergy
Severe reaction to certain types of food

Food group
Foods grouped according to their main nutritional content

FSA
Food Standards Agency

Healthy weight
Level of body fat that allows the body to function at its optimum potential

Hereditary
Passed on from parent to child

Insulin
Hormone produced by the pancreas necessary for carbohydrate metabolism

The International Obesity Taskforce (IOTF)
Part of the International Association for the Study of Obesity (IASO) is working with partners in the Global Prevention Alliance to support new strategies to improve diet and activity and prevent obesity and related chronic diseases with a special focus on preventing childhood obesity.

MEND
Mind, Exercise, Nutrition Do it programme

Monitoring
Regular checks and observations

Monounsaturated fat
Helps to improve cholesterol levels and prevent health risks.

NCMP
National Child Measurement Programme, which collects data on the height and weight of children in reception and Year 6

Nutrients
The building blocks of food, which provide physical growth and maintain a person's good health

NHSP
National Healthy Schools Programme

Obese
Grossly overweight with a BMI of 30kg/m2 or greater for adults and is age and gender dependent for children

Obesity
State of being well above one's normal weight

Overweight
A state between normal weight and obesity

Physical activity
Movement of the body produced by muscles contracting that cause energy expenditure

Polyunsaturated fat
Fat mainly from vegetable / plant sources, which may lower the level of blood cholesterol

Prevention
With regard to obesity, primary prevention represents avoiding the occurrence of obesity in a population; secondary prevention represents early detection of obesity through screening with the purpose of limiting its occurrence; and tertiary prevention involves preventing the cycle of obesity in childhood and adulthood

Primary Care Trusts (PCTs)
The Government departments that control local health care. There are PCTs covering all parts of England

Protein
Macronutrient essential for growth and repair of body tissue, which can be both animal and plant sourced

Saturated fat
Fat mainly from animal source, linked to coronary heart disease

Self-esteem
Belief in ones self

Unsaturated fat
Fats that help maintain a healthy heart (monounsaturated or polyunsaturated)

Vegan
A diet that excludes eating animal flesh and animal products

Vegetarian
A diet that excludes the eating of animal flesh

Vitamins
Essential substances that cannot be manufactured by the body, important for growth and development.

Weight loss
Decrease in body weight resulting from diet and exercise

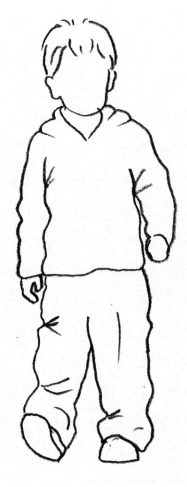

Useful addresses

British Nutrition Foundation (BNF)

52-54 High Holborn House
High Holborn
London
WC1V 6RQ
Tel: 020 7404 6504
Fax: 020 7404 6747
Email: postbox@nutrition.org.uk
www.nutrition.org.uk

Children Living with Inherited Metabolic Disease (CLIMB)

Climb Building
176 Nantwich Road
Crewe
CW2 6BG.
Tel: 0845 241 2172
Email: info.svcs@climb.org.uk
www.climb.org.uk

Children's Workforce Development Council (CWDC)

2nd Floor
City Exchange
11 Albion Street
Leeds
LS1 5ES
Tel: 0113 244 6311
Fax: 0113 390 7744

Department for Children, Schools and Families (DCSF)

Sanctuary Buildings
Great Smith Street
London
SW1P 3BT
Tel: 0870 000 2288
Fax: 01928 794248
Email: info@dcsf.gsi.gov.uk
www.dcsf.gov.uk

Department for Culture Media & Sport (DCMS)

2-4 Cockspur Street
London
SW1Y 5DH
Tel: 020 7211 6200
Email: enquiries@culture.gov.uk
www.culture.gov.uk

Department of Health (DH)

The Department of Health
Richmond House
79 Whitehall
London
SW1A 2NS
Tel: 020 7210 4850
Email: dhmail@dh.gsi.gov.uk
www.dh.gov.uk

Food Standards Agency (FSA)

Communication Division
2nd floor
Aviation House
125 Kingsway
London
WL2B 6NH
Tel: 020 7276 8829
Email: helpline@foodstandards.gsi.gov.uk
www.foodstandards.gov.uk

International Obesity Taskforce (IOTF)

28 Portland Place
London
W1B 1LY
Tel: +44 (0) 20 7691 1900
Fax: +44 (0) 20 7387 6033
Email: obesity@iotf.org
www.iotf.org/childhoodobesity.asp

Qualification and Curriculum Authority (QCA)

83 Piccadilly
London
W1J 8QA
Tel: 020 7509 5555
Fax: 020 7509 6666
Email: info@qca.org.uk
www.qca.uk

Word Health Organisation (WHO)

Avenue Appia 20
1211 Geneva 27
Switzerland
Tel: + 41 22 791 21 11
Fax: + 41 22 791 31 11
Email: info@who.int.
www.euro.who.int/obesity

Useful websites

Bullying UK
www.bullying.co.uk
Bullying UK provides information and advice for schools and parents on all matters of bullying.

Change 4 life
www.nhs.uk/change4life
The Change 4 Life website contains tons of helpful information for parents, games, tools, tips and a free welcome pack. Parents can search for what is happening in their local community. The site is updated regularly and outlines the government proposals for healthy living.

The Children's Plan: Building Brighter Futures, DCSF (2007)
www.dcsf.gov.uk/publications/childrensplan
Download a copy of The Children's Plan: Building Brighter Futures that explains how the Department for Children, Schools and Families aim to make the UK the best place in the world for children and young people to grow up, by putting the needs of families, children and young people at the centre of everything we do.

Food for Life
www.foodforlife.org.uk
Lottery funded organisation that plans to revolutionise school meals, reconnect young people with farms and inspire families to cook and grow food. It is possible to enrol your school for The Food for Life Partnership Mark, an action framework and award scheme that aims to help schools and their communities improve their food culture. If your school meals are supplied by a private contractor or local authority caterer you will need to get the support of your caterer to take part.

Children First for Health (CFfH)
www.childrenfirst.nhs.uk/kids/health/eat_smart/obesity_lowdown/index.html
Children first for Health, is a child-centred health and hospital resource, supporting teenagers, children and their families, produced by Great Ormond Street Hospital and the NHS. It provides comprehensive and age-appropriate health information from the UK's leading medical experts and paediatricians. There is a section on obesity and healthy eating.

Let's get cooking
www.letsgetcooking.org.uk/Howtheprogrammeworks/Whowantstogetcooking/Primaryschoolpupils
This website provides practical information on how to set up a cooking club in your school.

Licence to Cook
www.licencetocook.org.uk/cooking.aspx
The License to Cook website gives basic tutorials in cooking skills, eating, shopping and hygiene with online assessments for each section to test the children's knowledge.

National Child Measurement Programme
www.dh.gov.uk/en/Publichealth/Healthimprovement/Healthyliving/DH_073787
Department of Health website that gives detailed information about the National Child Measurement Programme and how it will help to increase public and professional understanding of weight issues in children.

National Healthy Schools Programme (NHSP)
www.healthyschools.gov.uk
The DCSF and NHS website provides information on the National Healthy Schools Programme, a long-term initiative which is making a significant difference to the health and achievement of children and young people.

The New Performance Framework for Local Authority Partnerships: Single Set of National Indicators
www.communities.gov.uk/publications/localgovernment/nationalindicator
Download a copy of the New Performance Framework for Local Authority Partnerships: Single Set of National Indicators. This publication is only available online.

The MEND Programme
www.mendprogramme.org
This website provides information about the MEND programme and how to join. This lottery funded initiative aims to help children become fitter, healthier and happier.

Million Meals campaign
www.millionmeals.schoolfoodtrust.org.uk
This is a School Food Trust site. Schools are able to sign up using the school's URN number to gain access to a panel of experts and champions who will be able to give insights into how they have transformed the school meal service and answer any queries.

National Obesity Forum
www.nationalobesityforum.org.uk
This is an excellent website that contains up-to-date information on obesity issues, recent research and news. The National Obesity Forum was established by medical practitioners in May 2000 to raise awareness of the growing health impact that being overweight or obese was having on patients and the National Health Service. They are an independent charity, working to improve the prevention and management of obesity.

National Sleep Foundation (NSF)
www.sleepfoundation.org
The National Sleep Foundation is an independent non-profit American organization dedicated to improving public health and safety by achieving understanding of sleep and sleep disorders. Find out more information on how sleep affects our health and a lack of sleep can cause weight gain.

Further reading

A Practical Guide to Child Nutrition
Angela Dare and *Margaret O'Donovan*
Nelson Thorne (2007)

Children's Health, Combating Child Obesity
Nicolette Heaton-Harris
Emerald Publishing (2007)

Detoxing Childhood: What Parents Need To Know To Raise Happy, Successful Children
Sue Palmer
Orion Books (2007)

Development of Food Acceptance Patterns in the First years of Life
L. S. Birch
Proceedings of the Nutrition Society 57,
no 4 (1998): 614-24

Establishing a standard definition for child overweight and obesity worldwide: international survey
T J Cole, M C Bellizzi, K M Flegal, W H Dietz
British Medical Journal, British Medical Association (2000)

From Kid to Superkid
Paul Sacher
Vermilion (2005)

Healthy weight, healthy lives: guidance for local areas
Cross Government Obesity Unit
DCSF (March 2007)

How to set and monitor goals for prevalence of child obesity: guidance for Primary Care Trusts (PCTs) and local authorities
Cross Government Obesity Unit
DCSF (Feb 2008)

Lightening the load: tackling overweight and obesity
Dr Kerry Swanton and Monica Frost
British Heart Forum (2007)

Obesity Guidance for Healthy Schools Coordinators and their Partners
DH/HID/Obesity – Healthy Schools Programme
Department of Health (Jan 2007)

Preventing Childhood Obesity
Jennifer Rice and Angela Sharpe
British Medical Association Board of Science
(June 2005)

The Future of Children: Spring 2006: Childhood Obesity
Christina Paxson, Elisabeth Donahue, Tracy Orleans, and Jeanne Ann Grisso
Princeton University US (2006)

They Are What You Feed Them
Alex Richardson
Harper Collins (2006)

Notes

Notes

Notes